THE
FUTURE

OF MISSIONS

**10 Questions About Global Ministry the Church
Must Answer with the Next Generation**

Produced in Partnership with the International Mission Board

ISBN: 978-1-945269-69-1

Funding for this research was made possible by the generous support of the International Mission Board. Barna Group was solely responsible for data collection, analysis and writing of the report.

Contents

Preface

BY DR. PAUL CHITWOOD

God's Spirit is moving in unprecedented ways around the world! The number of people groups not yet engaged with the gospel continues to decline. Nations once targeted for mission work are now sending out their own international missionaries. And even under the rule of governments hostile to Christianity, churches are multiplying by the thousands.

Yet, much work remains. According to our best estimates, 154,937 people in the world die every day without a saving faith in Jesus Christ. Many simply have never had an opportunity to hear the gospel—the good news of salvation in Jesus—in their heart language in a way they can understand it.

Alongside such great movement and great need around the world, news from North America seems grim: Church attendance—and the number of Americans who identify as Christians—is in sharp decline. Younger Christians report they don't prioritize church involvement in their lives. Nearly half of young adults don't think Jesus' mandate to "go and make disciples" applies to them.

At the International Mission Board (IMB), our mission is to serve Southern Baptists in carrying out the Great Commission to make disciples of all nations. Our very existence for the past 175 years has pointed to the promise that, one day, there will be "a multitude from every language, people, tribe and nation knowing and worshiping our Lord Jesus Christ" (Revelation 7:9–10, *ESV*). That is a big promise, and it's also a big challenge.

As the largest missionary-sending agency of our kind, we're compelled to search for solutions to the challenges of a declining missionary candidate pipeline and a plateaued giving stream. We can no longer expect that future generations of Protestants will inherently engage in missions education and missions action. We're obliged to ask the hard questions: *How do we bridge the gap between shrinking church attendance and a burgeoning world population that doesn't have access to the gospel? How does the next generation contribute to fulfilling this spectacular vision so beautifully revealed in Revelation?*

In essence: *What is the future of missions?*

We're thankful for the insights this work with Barna is uncovering and confirming, presented as 10 questions about global ministry the Church must answer with the next generation. This report considers what Christian parents and church leaders are seeing in our young adults: Christianity is being marginalized as "extreme," consumerism and self-fulfillment are taking center stage and young people feel increasingly uneasy about the idea of evangelism.

Given these realities, the findings reported here uncover the next generation's opinions on how we should talk about missions, how we should fund missions and what role aid or compassion ministry plays in missions.

As the largest missionary-sending agency of our kind, we're obliged to ask the hard questions

As parents, we can learn how we are sometimes a barrier to missions engagement (we're very supportive of *someone else's kid* serving overseas!), but also discover ways we can encourage our children if they feel led into short-term or long-term missions service. One encouraging note is that the teens and young adults interviewed say they *do* care about their parents' opinions!

We think you'll also be encouraged as church leaders to know how you can influence the future of missions. The data show an exponential increase in a person's praying for missions, giving to missions and going on long-term missions if they've met a missionary personally, had a short-term mission experience or had some other missions involvement. Your commitment to enlisting a missionary to interact with younger generations in your church, and your drive to help young people engage in missions service, will impact generations to come.

My hope is that through the research presented in this report, you'll discover insights that can inform your family, church or sending organization how to stretch and adjust to stay on mission. The news may seem grim. But the future is bright. We know how the story ends— we've read the final chapter.

Let's step into the future of missions together.

DR. PAUL CHITWOOD was elected president of IMB in November 2018. He previously served as executive director of the Kentucky Baptist Convention. For 18 years, he was the pastor of local churches of varying sizes. His overseas short-term mission involvement includes work in South America, Asia, Europe and Africa. A native of Jellico, Tennessee, Chitwood is a graduate of Cumberland College and the Southern Baptist Theological Seminary.

Introduction

When Marion and James went as missionaries in 1990 to train pastors in East Africa, they felt a nascent sense of the globe's *smallness*. The Berlin Wall had fallen just a few months earlier—an event they had watched together on nightly network news—and the unfolding of history right before their eyes made them feel that the world was getting smaller.

Small as the world was becoming, however, international telephone service was unreliable and prohibitively expensive, and they couldn't chat very often with friends and family back in the U.S. News in the country where they served was government-owned and -controlled, making it sometimes hard to know the facts of events close by and back at home. James wrote fundraising letters long hand and Marion painstakingly typed them up on an IBM Selectric, then air-mailed the one and only hard copy to a stateside friend—who, two to four weeks later, mimeographed it, stuffed the smeary black-and-white copies into envelopes and mailed them to churches across North America.

That was 30 years ago.

In one of those churches was a little girl named Tasha. One of her earliest memories is of her mom teaching her how to pray for "our missionaries," Miss Marion and Reverend James, whose picture card hung on the refrigerator alongside snapshots of family members and artwork Tasha brought home from school.

By the time she was 12 years old, Tasha subscribed to Marion and James's monthly e-newsletter and started an email correspondence with a girl her own age in the East African city where they made their home. When she was 16, Tasha went with her dad on a two-week mission trip hosted by Marion and James. It changed the course of her life. She sensed God calling her to mission work, and every choice after that—what college to attend, what guy to date—was made with missions in mind.

Serving today on the mission field as a Hebrew teacher for young Bible scholars and as an app developer for rural entrepreneurs who want to expand their markets, Tasha can send text, audio and video messages from her mobile phone that friends and family receive immediately. She checks and compares trusted news websites from around the world to construct a fairly accurate picture of local and international events. She instantly updates supporters from multiple countries who follow her on social media.

She can receive and send money, make and modify travel plans, video call her boyfriend or a supporting church, meet with fellow Bible scholars on different continents, order needed supplies for delivery to almost any location on earth and watch the new season of *The Great British Baking Show*.

Thanks to mobile technology and global connectivity, the world has gotten very small indeed.

Missions for the 21st Century

Technology is not the only thing that has transformed the context of missions. Attitudes toward Christianity have also shifted.

Thanks to mobile technology and global connectivity, the world has gotten very small indeed

After returning from that life-altering missions trip, Tasha presented a report to her world history class about the Kenyan fight for independence from Great Britain, won in December 1963. The teacher gave her a *B* because Tasha "left out how Western missionaries gave moral cover to the colonials." This was partly true, as a disillusioned Tasha found when she did more research on the subject—but it wasn't the *whole* truth. Christian missionaries in mid-century Kenya ran the gamut from hardcore colonial collaborators to spies for the freedom fighters and everything in between; most, for better or worse, focused on their local work and prayed the national situation would be resolved as peacefully as possible.[1] Thanks to her teacher's cynicism, Tasha learned more about the complex history of mission-sending from the global North—including what *not* to do, in order to be the kind of missionary she wants to be.

David Kinnaman, Barna's president, has documented shifting attitudes toward faith in books like *unChristian, You Lost Me* and *Good Faith,* in which he shows evidence that Americans—in particular, younger Americans—are growing increasingly skeptical about religious people. Many public expressions of faith are looked upon with mistrust or even hostility. As an example, eight out of 10 U.S. adults who are religiously unaffiliated (sometimes called "nones") say that sharing one's faith in hopes the other person will convert is "extreme" (83%).[2]

There are a lot of young Christians like Tasha—not necessarily called to serve overseas, but aware of Christianity's conflicted past and determined to live their faith differently. Barna has gotten to know young Jesus followers through a variety of metrics, including faith practices, specific beliefs, views on social issues and, in Kinnaman's book *Faith for Exiles,* faith resiliency—that is, how well faith holds up over time and through various stages of life.

Engaged Christian faith is alive among Millennials and Gen Z, but there's also no doubt that the overall percentage of engaged Christians (see definitions on page 14) is shrinking in each successive generation: 22 percent among Boomers, 18 percent among Gen X, 12 percent among Millennials.[3] This matters for many reasons, but when it comes to missions the probable outcomes are stark: Even if every single young engaged Christian were just as supportive of international ministry as older believers, there are fewer of them to sustain missions into the future. This has profound implications not just for the spread of the good news about Christ but also for the humanitarian work carried out in his name. Numerous studies have shown that religious people give more and volunteer more than their irreligious counterparts, and not only to faith-based causes.[4] With fewer and fewer Christians to support them, what will become of life-saving mission hospitals, midwife training schools and freshwater well builders? And what if some of the Christians in the next generation aren't convinced of the necessity of missions?

As we will see in *The Future of Missions* data, not all young engaged Christians are on board.

Some are grappling with how missions has been done and wondering if it's the best we can do.

Some are thinking about the donations model of missionary funding and imagining 21st-century alternatives.

Some are waking up to the social justice implications of cross-cultural ministry and reassessing their assumptions about evangelism.

Many are traveling to other countries and connecting on social media with people from other cultures, religions, political persuasions and ideologies—and allowing their experiences and conversations to inform their ideas about living as a Christian in an ever-smaller, multicultural world.

Asking the Right Questions About Missions

Given all these cultural realities, the International Mission Board of

> There are a lot of young Christians who are aware of Christianity's conflicted past and are determined to live their faith differently

the Southern Baptist Convention commissioned Barna to find out how young Christians' perspectives on missions are different from older believers'—and what these differences might mean for the next chapter of the Church's global mission, not just for IMB but for everyone. Researchers designed a study among engaged Protestants ages 13 and older, with slightly different surveys for teens, young adults 18 to 34 and adults 35 and older. (Read all the details in the Methodology on page 107.)

In this report, Barna has distilled our findings down to 10 vital questions for the Church—questions that can't be answered without the next generation. *The Future of Missions* examines each of these questions, and the data behind them, in turn. Along the way, we'll get to know current missionaries in various parts of the world and hear about their experiences, priorities, hopes and struggles (names and some details have been changed to protect their families and ministries). We'll also hear from people connected to missions in different ways—parents, sending organizations, former missionaries—to get a multifaceted view of missions today.

As we explore the findings together, we hope you'll sense God's Spirit calling *you* to join the conversation.

About the Research

Barna designed quantitative surveys to study the pipeline for future missions engagement, focusing primarily on teens (600) and young adults (1,200), including those actively engaged in a church as well as those committed to faith but who may not be part of a physical church community. Older engaged churchgoing adults (1,500) were surveyed for comparison to younger generations, but also to explore how they might further support or even participate in missions. Barna also surveyed 500 engaged Christian parents of teens and young adults to explore how their influence directly or indirectly impacts their children's engagement with missions.

Definitions

Engaged churchgoing Christians, sometimes called *engaged Christians* in this report for the sake of brevity, attend a Protestant church at least once a month, say they are involved with their church in more ways than just attending services, have made a commitment to Jesus that is important in their life today and say their religious faith is very important in their life today. Age groups:

- Teens 13 to 17
- Young adults 18 to 34
- Older adults 35 and older

Other engaged Christians, sometimes called *non-churchgoers* in this report, otherwise qualify as engaged but are not regular churchgoers.

Engaged Christian parents are engaged Christians who have at least one child age 13 to 25.

Potential missionaries say they would "definitely" be interested in serving as one or more of four different missionary profiles (see ch. 8).

Ethnicity is based on self-identification.

Supportive skeptics:

- Have donated money to missions
- Don't think missionary work is "very" valuable *or* are bothered by evangelism
- Agree strongly or somewhat with one or more of the following statements:
  - Missions work can sometimes lead to unhealthy local dependence on charity.
  - Charity work often hurts the local economy.
  - Christianity should fix its reputation before doing more missions.
  - Christian mission is tainted by its association with colonialism.

Seven out of 10 engaged churchgoing Christians in every age cohort consider missionary work "very valuable."

Young black Christians 18 to 34 are less likely than the white majority to call missions very valuable (62% vs. 73%), yet they are *more* likely to be potential missionaries (61% vs. 48%).

Relatedly, more Christians 18 to 34 than older adults express concern about missions' past. One-third agrees that "in the past, mission work has been unethical" (34%) compared to about one in four adults 35+ (22%).

Key Findings

Even so, half of young Christians 18 to 34 (52%) qualify as potential missionaries compared to just 28 percent of older adults.

Young Christians who know a missionary are more likely to say they will give to missions (58% vs. 46% don't know a missionary), pray for missionaries (54% vs. 45%) and go on a short-term (40% vs. 30%) or long-term (22% vs. 9%) missions trip.

Three out of four engaged Christian parents say they are at least somewhat open to their child becoming a missionary (35% very, 39% somewhat).

What Do People Value About International Missions?

Missionaries do all kinds of jobs. In just the small sample of current missionaries Barna profiled for this project, there are an artist, a dentist, a pastor, a writer, a graphic designer, a midwife, a farmer, several educators and a tech entrepreneur, among others. These missionaries do everything from producing shareable videos for nonprofit organizations in Asia to helping sex workers escape forced prostitution in Europe, from teaching sustainable land management to subsistence farmers in East Africa to managing a neighborhood art gallery and studio in Berlin. The common denominator among these enormously varied job functions is a calling to work on behalf of God's Kingdom outside one's home culture. No matter their job, they are all missionaries.

There is a stereotype, however, that has taken hold in the North American cultural imagination, of a "white savior" evangelist who exports their narrow, Western-centric version of faith with more passion

CHAPTER

1

than cultural competence. (Like many stereotypes, this one is based on a minority whose actions and attitudes have tainted missionaries' overall public image.) One representative opinion from a Millennial African American woman has been retweeted, as of this writing, more than 6,000 times—suggesting that many young adults are ready to sign off on the sentiment: "Missionary work is a form of colonization and inherently racist."[5]

Most engaged Christians of any age have had enough exposure to real-life missionaries that they don't buy into this mindset—and in fact, those who are 18 to 34 are more likely than teens and older adults to say they personally know at least one missionary "well" (58% vs. 47% adults 35 and older, 36% teens 13 to 17). But how much do they actually know about what missionaries do? Do they value what they suppose missionaries do, however much they know? Are there differences in how older and younger Christians feel about missionary work?

When researchers ask about the value of overseas ministry, a strong majority of engaged Christians in every generation says missionary work is "very valuable." Statistically speaking, the three age cohorts are indistinguishable.

"Missionary Work Is Very Valuable"

% very

● Teens 13–17　● Young adults 18–34　● Older adults 35+

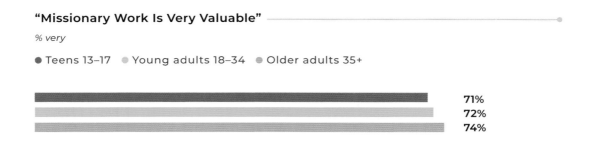

71%
72%
74%

n=U.S. engaged churchgoing Christians: 1,500 adults 35 and older, 856 adults 18 to 34, 464 teens 13 to 17, Dec. 2018–Jan. 2019.

Among Americans under 35, however, black engaged Christians (61% teens, 62% young adults) are more reluctant than the white majority (74% teens, 73% young adults) to say they value missionaries' work. (The difference between blacks and whites in the older cohort is not statistically significant.) Given the Euro-American Church's historical entanglements with colonialism and African slavery, and the growing cultural awareness of that legacy's ongoing impact, it's not surprising that young black Americans would express deeper ambivalence. (Check out the Q&A with Barbara Jones on page 30 for more insights on this vital thread of the missions conversation.)

Young Christians still value what missionaries do but, as we will see, many also have significant and often valid questions about the *why* and *how* of international missions. In fact, analysts found a group of engaged Christians that both expresses reservations and, at the same time, either financially supports a missionary or has been on at least one overseas mission trip themselves (both, for most people in this population). So their reservations are not based on hearsay or cultural zeitgeist but on their own informed engagement with missions. Barna calls them "**supportive skeptics**," and our team believes they will play an important role in the unfolding story of missions' future—and so they pop up throughout this report, as we try to understand together where global missions is headed. (The Q&A with Erin and Julian Williams on page 62 is a snapshot of two supportive skeptics.) One in four engaged Christians ages 18 to 34 (26%) is a supportive skeptic, compared to one in five adults 35 and older (19%) and one in five teens (21%). Among young adults in particular, ethnic minorities are over-represented among supportive skeptics.

What Missionaries Do

Researchers offered survey participants a list of ministry job functions and asked them whether missionaries always, sometimes or never do that job. Using the same list, respondents could then judge if missionaries always, sometimes or never *should* do that job. ("I don't know" was also an option, and teen respondents, in particular, were often not shy about admitting their ignorance.) "Show other people God's love" comes out on top of both the "missionaries do" and the "should do" list among all three age cohorts—so there is broad agreement among Christians that showing God's love is and should be missionaries' main task. But looking at the gaps between "do" and "should" for some of the remaining tasks can help us get a handle on young adults' views and attitudes toward missionary work.

Young Adults on What Missionaries Do vs. What They *Should* Do

% "always"

● Missionaries do ● Missionaries should

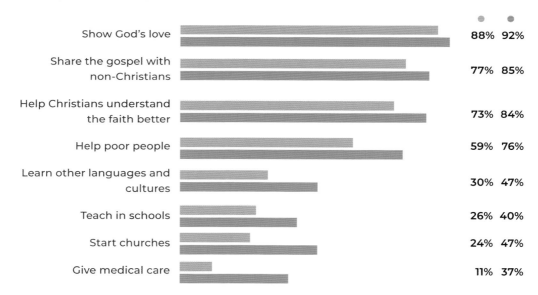

	Do	Should
Show God's love	88%	92%
Share the gospel with non-Christians	77%	85%
Help Christians understand the faith better	73%	84%
Help poor people	59%	76%
Learn other languages and cultures	30%	47%
Teach in schools	26%	40%
Start churches	24%	47%
Give medical care	11%	37%

n=856 U.S. engaged churchgoing Christians 18 to 34, Dec. 2018–Jan. 2019.

Young adults, by and large, support these missionary functions, in line with older adult and teen engaged Christians. Notice, however, that the three tasks with the biggest difference between "missionaries do" and "missionaries should" each have a social justice component: access that is otherwise not available to underserved communities (medical care), and affirming (learn language and culture) and empowering indigenous Christians (start churches). As we've seen in previous Barna studies among Millennials and Gen Z, the high value they place on justice can complicate young Christians' views of global missions and ministry in general.

Young Christians value what missionaries do, but many also have significant and often valid questions about the *why* and *how* of missions

For example, a significant minority of young engaged Christians sees missionary work as inseparable from social justice work. Three in 10 (29%) say a missionary and "someone else

Getting Local

Devin and Helena, along with their kids, serve with IMB in a majority-Muslim city in Africa as a school administrator and a medical volunteer. They each sensed a call to missions and served as solo missionaries before they married. They've been on the field more than 10 years, and their focus is on forming and deepening friendships with families in their community. This is a challenge not only because of cultural and religious differences but also because of urban population churn: People are constantly coming and going, whether because of political unrest or in search of better economic and educational opportunities for themselves and their children.

Devin and Helena both favor local missionary employment—that is, having a job in the community where one serves, participating in the local economy—rather than living solely on (or perhaps in addition to) outside financial support. They love raising their kids overseas because it gives them "a more complete global context" for their growing faith and long-term future.

who does work to fight poverty and injustice" are *very similar*, compared to about one-quarter of older Christians (23%)—and they're *less* likely than older adults to say these two types of international workers are *not very* or *not at all similar* (17% vs. 24% adults 35+). That is, older engaged Christians are more likely than young adults to see a bright line between missionaries' work and that of aid or humanitarian workers.

Is there a difference? Should there be? Who can and should address these questions?

MISSIONS & YOU

- Do you value missions work? Why or why not? What would you say to someone who answers differently?

- What do you think missionaries should do? As you consider the future of missions, are there some things they definitely *shouldn't* do? Why?

- Do you know a missionary? What do you know about how they spend their days? How do you feel about what you know? What do you wish you knew more about? (If you don't know a missionary, you likely know someone who does and could help you get connected.)

How Does Missions' History Shape Its Present & Future?

Although there are many examples of the transformative value of missionary work around the world, there are also aspects of its history—and sometimes its present—that are difficult or even impossible to defend. Anyone who dreams and plans for the missionary future must grapple with these realities.

Overall, engaged churchgoing Christians 18 to 34 appear to be more concerned than older adults with problematic aspects of the past. (It's worth mentioning here that, in Barna's experience, teen responses often look like their parents'; when they move into young adulthood, however, their views start to diverge more from previous generations' as they form their own opinions.) One-third of young adult Christians (34%) agrees that "in the past, missions work has been unethical," compared to one in four adults 35 and older (23%). Two in five (42%) agree that "Christian mission is tainted by its association with colonialism" (vs. 29% adults 35+, 31% teens).

CHAPTER

2

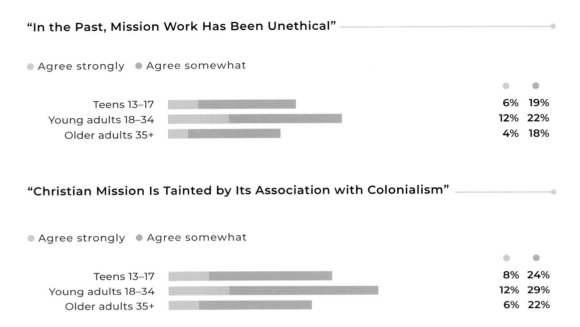

"In the Past, Mission Work Has Been Unethical"

● Agree strongly ● Agree somewhat

	●	●
Teens 13–17	6%	19%
Young adults 18–34	12%	22%
Older adults 35+	4%	18%

"Christian Mission Is Tainted by Its Association with Colonialism"

● Agree strongly ● Agree somewhat

	●	●
Teens 13–17	8%	24%
Young adults 18–34	12%	29%
Older adults 35+	6%	22%

n=U.S. engaged churchgoing Christians: 1,500 adults 35 and older, 856 adults 18 to 34, 464 teens 13 to 17, Dec. 2018–Jan. 2019.

Supportive skeptics—that is, engaged Christians who don't consider missionary work "very valuable" but nonetheless are engaged in giving to or going on mission—seem to be more concerned than others about the shameful parts of mission history. This is true for supportive skeptics in all three age cohorts, but most of all among young adults. (See charts on opposite page.)

Many of these same engaged young believers say Christianity should rehabilitate its reputation before continuing international missions work.

Supportive Skeptics

● Agree strongly ● Agree somewhat

"In The Past, Missions Work Has Been Unethical"

	●	●
Teens 13–17	12%	33%
Young adults 18–34	16%	35%
Older adults 35+	5%	37%

"Christian Mission Is Tainted by Its Association with Colonialism"

	●	●
Teens 13–17	11%	39%
Young adults 18–34	18%	53%
Older adults 35+	8%	41%

"Christianity Should Fix Its Reputation Before Doing More Missions"

	●	●
Teens 13–17	9%	41%
Young adults 18–34	18%	45%
Older adults 35+	14%	37%

n=U.S. engaged churchgoing Christian supportive skeptics: 290 adults 35 and older, 310 adults 18 to 34, 125 teens 13 to 17, Dec. 2018–Jan. 2019.

Calling More People of Color

Bren, who is white, and her husband, Jos, who is black, are new to the field and are serving with IMB in Johannesburg. They long to see more people of color answer God's call to missions. "Like it or not, African Americans have an advantage as missionaries in Africa in terms of trust," Bren says. "There is a perception that Christianity is a white religion, a tool of oppression. As a minority white person here, I often feel I'm either automatically distrusted or given unearned respect. It's really hard to get past that to make real friendships."

Jos says, "There is a tiny number of African Americans being sent as missionaries, probably less than two percent. I am the exception. I didn't even know being a missionary was something black people did! It's hard to be called to something if you don't see any examples you can relate to. But then I started to catch a vision of people who look like me doing this work. I started to understand, *God really does desire to use you and your people. There is a place for you. Your gifts, perspectives and experiences are invaluable. You don't have to lose your blackness.*"

What Young Christians Would Change

Among the one in 10 engaged Christian young adults who tell researchers they would change something specific about missions work (10% vs. 8% adults 35+, 7% teens), more than one-third are supportive skeptics (35%). Dealing with the past is a common theme. They want to support missionaries who are aware of their own biases and committed to respecting other cultures, even if that means more emphasis on aid or justice work and less "pushiness"—more than one respondent used this word—about sharing the gospel. (Read more about perceived tension between evangelism and humanitarian work in chapter 4.)

Relatedly, some who name specific changes they would make to missions point to potential deleterious effects on missionaries' character and spiritual life. One former MK (missionary's kid) commented on Facebook, "Putting human beings in a context where they are always 'special' and celebrated, at home and in the field, is spiritually destructive to self and others. It breeds narcissism and can have far-reaching negative effects. Obviously not everyone falls into this trap but those who aren't self-aware and vigilant inevitably do."[6]

Others express a desire to change the traditional donations-based funding model (more on that in chapter 5) or want better accountability and consistent communication from missionaries (see chapter 6). And still other engaged Christian young adults articulate some level of unease about short-term missions in particular. "They benefit the people going more than the ones we are serving," commented one mom. "I don't know if that is all bad, but I really question how much good we do when we go." A young graphic artist agrees: "Our tendency to make overseas trips about OUR experience (or lack of it) and OUR imposition into cultures and communities that we don't have a stake in really makes this kind of missionary work seem out of touch and time to me." On the other hand, says a 30-something Michigan pastor with a missions background, "If done in partnership with local churches, [short-term missions] can be fruitful for those who are going and those who are in the local community. It is essential that people go as learners and not experts. We have so many things to learn from our international brothers and sisters in Christ."

Among the young Christians who would change something about missions, dealing with the past is a common theme

MISSIONS & YOU

- How well or poorly do you think the Church in the global North is dealing with its past? What can you do to help God's people in this task?

- What would *you* change about missions?

- What do you think about short-term missions? If you have concerns, what are your ideas for making short-term trips better for everyone involved?

Getting to Know Young Supportive Skeptics

The unique group whom Barna calls "supportive skeptics"* is intriguing because they appear to care deeply about the work of Christ and his Church in the world, but also feel at least some measure of conflict about how missions has been done. Getting to know the young supportive skeptics in your community is crucial: Their passion for the gospel and eagerness to support just and culture-honoring ways of doing cross-cultural ministry are desperately needed in the global Church.

One in Four Engaged Christian Young Adults Is a Supportive Skeptic

- Teens 13–17
- Young adults 18–34
- Older adults 35+

- 21%
- 26%
- 19%

People of Color Ages 18 to 34 Are More Likely Than Average to Be Supportive Skeptics

- White
- Black
- Hispanic
- Asian

Supportive skeptics
- 64%
- 26%
- 15%
- 5%†

All other engaged Christian young adults
- 69%
- 19%
- 10%
- 6%

They Are Still Evangelistically Inclined

What should missionaries do?

% always

- Supportive skeptics
- All other engaged Christian young adults

	Supportive skeptics	All other engaged Christian young adults
Show other people God's love	88%	93%
Help Christians understand the faith better	76%	86%
Share the gospel with non-Christians	76%	88%

*Supportive skeptics have donated money to missions and either don't think missionary work is "very valuable" or are bothered by evangelism. In addition, they agree with one or more of the following statements: (1) Missions work can sometimes lead to unhealthy local dependence on charity; (2) Charity work often hurts the local economy; (3) Christianity should fix its reputation before doing more missions; (4) Christian mission is tainted by its association with colonialism.

...But Also Deeply Concerned About the Ethics of Missions

% agree

	●	●
"In the past, missions work has been unethical"	51%	29%
"Missions work can sometimes lead to unhealthy local dependence on charity"	66%	35%
"Christianity should fix its reputation before doing more missions"	63%	31%
"Christian mission is tainted by its association with colonialism"	71%	32%

They're Active in Their Faith & More Likely Than Others to Volunteer

% within the past week

	●	●
Attended church	78%	82%
Read the Bible	79%	81%
Attended a small group	61%	56%
Volunteered at church	56%	50%
Volunteered for a nonprofit	33%	26%
Attended Sunday school	57%	52%

● Supportive skeptics   ○ All other engaged Christian young adults

Business leader   Artist   Church trainer   Entrepreneur

They're as Willing as Others to Consider Serving in a Missionary Role *% definitely*

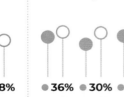

● 29%	● 27%	● 27%	● 28%
○ 31%	○ 32%	○ 34%	○ 33%

...But Not as Open to Giving Financial Support

% definitely

● 36%	● 30%	● 37%	● 31%
○ 40%	○ 40%	○ 47%	○ 39%

When Talking About Missionary Work, Supportive Skeptics ...

Still resonate with terms like:
(% like)

"Sharing faith"	60%	58%
"Missions"	28%	18%
"Missionary work"	28%	23%

...But they don't like:
(% dislike)

"Convert"	41%	33%
"Winning souls"	36%	29%
"Making disciples"	20%	12%

n=633 U.S. engaged Christians defined as supportive skeptics (99 teens, 228 ages 18–34, 306 ages 35 and older), Dec. 2018–Jan. 2019.
†Totals do not equal 100% because respondents could select all that apply.

Sending Missionaries of Every Color to Every Tribe & Nation

Q&A WITH BARBARA JONES, SENIOR NATIONAL DIVERSITY MOBILIZER FOR MISSION TO THE WORLD

Q Millennials and now Gen Z are the most ethnically diverse generations in U.S. history. Is the missionary workforce likewise diversifying? Why is this important?

A Mission-sending agencies realize how urgent it is to mobilize the next generation of missionaries, including Millennials and Gen Z. Many also want to incorporate strategies to raise up more diverse missionaries. But the workforce is diversifying at an extremely slow pace—sometimes because the sending agency lacks cross-cultural competencies, sometimes because they haven't developed opportunities for younger leaders or are not equipped to develop younger leaders, sometimes because they need to evaluate and revamp their systems and structures. We have to be honest with ourselves and make desperately needed changes if we want to raise up the next generation of laborers for the harvest.

BARBARA D. JONES serves as a consultant to and on behalf of Mission to the World (MTW). She assists in leading mobilization efforts toward diversity and aids the broader Church in developing cultural competencies. After serving with Cru's "Here's Life Inner City" ministry and with the Evangelical Covenant Church, the Lord broadened her thinking about local and global missions by calling her to serve with World Relief, where Jones developed "Walk in My Shoes: A Refugee Experience." From there she came to MTW, where she assisted in redesigning the missionary assessment process. For over 24 years, she has coached, trained and discipled parishioners and missionaries and has led mission teams around the world. Jones is passionate about the need for the Church to create space through discipleship for the next generation of diverse laborers. She is married to Ernest T. Jones and is a mother and grandmother.

Q Barna found that Christians of color in younger generations are somewhat more skeptical of international missions than white believers. What are some ways that people of color can help the whole Christian community reckon with our past and move faithfully into the future?

A In many of our American mission sending agency contexts, some level of assimilation or tokenism has been required of people of color. That is, in order to participate in the mission, we had to speak like, dress like, sing songs like and express theology like majority culture. Over time, that assimilation has created missed opportunities for white majority culture to know us as complete and whole image-bearers of God who have beautifully diverse ways of living out, experiencing and expressing the gospel.

Millennial and Gen Z Christians have watched older generations—many of us for good and godly reasons—give up or stifle important parts of ourselves. They understand the cost, and many are refusing to be so compliant, choosing not to serve in and thereby perpetuate painful systems. And these systems become ever more irrelevant to them, as witnessed by their increasing distance from Christian institutions.

I long for a day when people of color can authentically and unapologetically bring our whole selves to the missions table. As people made in the *imago Dei*, we, by God's grace, bring unique and needed gifts to his Kingdom. And for such a time as this, many of us offer a prophetic voice that can aid his Body in reaching local and global contexts in ways that broaden Kingdom work. This would require all of us to:

- **Honestly address fears.** *What is keeping us from accepting people of color as equal image bearers?* History is one thing that impacts our ability to do this.

- **Develop cultural competencies.** *Do we believe our way of doing things is or should be "the norm"?* We must be willing to look in the mirror and address issues of power and control—and then make room for others.

- **Be humble enough to be discipled.** *Are we being led or taught by a person of color?* Marginalized people have essential wisdom for growing into Christlikeness when it comes to things like a theology of suffering, cross-cultural adaptation, dependence on God, discipleship and so on. As a Church on mission, we need this wisdom!

Q What do you say to a young person who expresses reservations about global missions, especially when it comes to respecting other cultures?

A If they are a fellow person of color expressing reservations, I say, "I totally understand." I acknowledge that colonialism in missions is real. But the mission of the Church remains, however imperfectly it has been implemented in the past.

In my experience, many young Christians have more first-hand experience engaging other cultures; there is at least a willingness to learn. Many have not only found themselves directly engaging with various cultures; they also live in a digitally diverse space where they encounter diversity every minute. While there is always room for growth, accepting and respecting different cultures is often welcomed by this generation—which is all the more reason the Church needs them to take up the mantle of missions.

How Should We Talk
& Pray About Missions?

R eligious language changes over time. Once-common words and phrases fall out of fashion and use for various reasons, often because younger generations feel their parents' and grandparents' preferred words don't adequately describe their experience. It was perfectly normal for young Christians in the 1980s to talk about "getting saved" or "being born again," for example—and while these phrases are still part and parcel of American evangelicalism, when was the last time you texted a friend about getting saved?

For years the Barna team has tracked attitudes toward religious language, especially words and phrases associated with Christianity. Findings published in *Reviving Evangelism* and *Spiritual Conversations in the Digital Age* indicate that younger generations of believers are more cautious than older Christians about how and when they use words like "evangelism" and "conversion."[7]

The Future of Missions data bolsters this evidence and, further, suggests that younger Christians' caution may be trickling upward, as it were. Researchers asked the three survey groups to choose their top two preferences from a list of terms related to missions. Across the board, "sharing faith" comes out on top, while preference for a more straight-forwardly religious option like "evangelism" falls parallel to age.

Engaged Christians are not alone in their discomfort. In Barna's missionary interviews, a desire to tread lightly when it comes to language came up a number of times. A Europe-based artist, for example, said, "In America I call myself a missionary, but not here. Here I'm an artist and a social worker. I do community development work. My story includes my faith, but I don't lead with that."

It's not a matter of embarrassment or shame. In some places in the world, calling oneself a missionary isn't merely socially awkward; it's

Preferred Terms Related to Missions

Respondents could choose two.

● Teens 13–17   ● Young adults 18–34   ● Older adults 35+

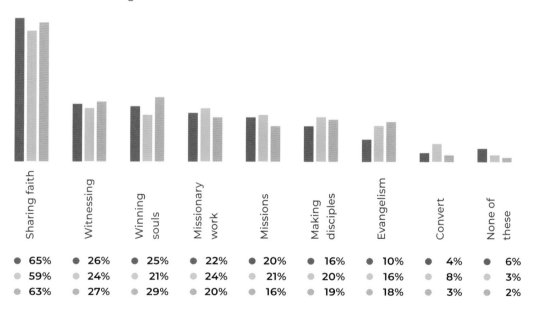

	Sharing faith	Witnessing	Winning souls	Missionary work	Missions	Making disciples	Evangelism	Convert	None of these
●	65%	26%	25%	22%	20%	16%	10%	4%	6%
●	59%	24%	21%	24%	21%	20%	16%	8%	3%
●	63%	27%	29%	20%	16%	19%	18%	3%	2%

n=U.S. engaged churchgoing Christians: 1,500 adults 35 and older, 856 adults 18 to 34, 464 teens 13 to 17, Dec. 2018–Jan. 2019.

a closed door. According to a seminary professor who trains aspiring missionaries, "There are places where you cannot get an entry visa to be a missionary. If you put 'missionary' on your visa request, it's denied. End of story."

Even in the U.S. where that's decidedly not the case, younger generations' dislike for what cynics sometimes call "Christianese" is obvious when they're asked what options they do *not* prefer when it comes to missions-related vocabulary. While a plurality of engaged Christians 35 and older (44%) says "none of these" options is troubling, "convert" tops the objectionable list for both young adults (35%) and teens (38%). Three in 10 (31% young adults, 30% teens) also reject "winning souls."

Objectionable Terms Related to Missions

Respondents could select all that apply.

● Teens 13–17 ● Young adults 18–34 ● Older adults 35+

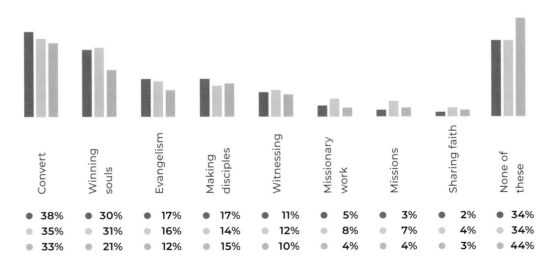

	Convert	Winning souls	Evangelism	Making disciples	Witnessing	Missionary work	Missions	Sharing faith	None of these
●	38%	30%	17%	17%	11%	5%	3%	2%	34%
●	35%	31%	16%	14%	12%	8%	7%	4%	34%
●	33%	21%	12%	15%	10%	4%	4%	3%	44%

n=U.S. engaged churchgoing Christians: 1,500 adults 35 and older, 856 adults 18 to 34, 464 teens 13 to 17, Dec. 2018–Jan. 2019.

Tentmaking, Not Tent-Faking

Allen was a church planter for 12 years but over time felt called into the financial sector to focus on what's sometimes called "business as mission." Now, in his words, he goes "wherever jobs and Jesus are needed." Most recently, that's in a city in Africa.

When he's not raising capital for a faith-based microfinance development NGO, Allen trains missionaries to be good businesspeople. "When 'business as mission' first started," he says, "we just dressed missionaries up in business attire. They weren't tentmakers; they were tent-fakers." Part of Allen's calling is to change that.

His other main focus is to inspire, recruit, equip and release ("dream-lease," as he calls it) established professionals onto the mission field. "People who have spent their lives getting MBAs and running great companies are no longer second-class Christians, but can have an immediate Kingdom impact."

Young Christians who are uncomfortable with missions language are often ready to engage *practically* but hesitant to do so *emotionally*

Listening intentionally to young Christians who object to at least one missions term uncovers important nuance: Their objections *don't* inevitably lead to disengagement from missions altogether. In fact, young adults who may squirm at the use of "convert" or "winning souls," for instance, are more likely than others to personally know a missionary (83% vs. 77%) and to have been on an international missions trip (41 vs. 29%). They are just as likely as others to say giving to and praying for missionaries (more on this soon) is in their future. At the same time, however, they are more likely to be supportive skeptics (30% vs. 18%) and to be troubled when it comes to the ethics of past missions efforts (39% agree vs. 25%).

Where does that leave them? They are often ready to engage *practically* with missions, but sometimes hesitant to *emotionally* engage.

Praying for Missionaries

Among engaged Protestants, younger generations' caution surrounding religious language isn't surprising, but researchers were somewhat taken off guard by their comparative disinterest in prayer. A strong majority of older adults (63%) says that in the future they see themselves praying specifically for missionaries, while only half of young adults (50%) and teens (51%) say so.

Analysts were surprised because engaged Christians under 35 are just as likely as their over-35 counterparts to report having prayed in the past seven days (within the margin of error, virtually 100%), and most have a regular prayer practice akin to older believers' habits. So the hindrance here seems to be prayer specifically for missionaries.

MISSIONS & YOU

- What words do you prefer when it comes to missions? What words do you *not* prefer? Why?

- Any ideas about what factors are at work in teens' and young adults' comparative reluctance to pray for missionaries? In your experience, why might they be less enthusiastic?

- Do you think it's important to pray for missionaries? What would you say to someone who thinks differently on this question?

"Praying for Missionaries Is in My Future"

% who select this from a list of options

● Teens 13–17 ● Young adults 18–34 ● Older adults 35+

▬▬▬▬▬▬▬▬▬▬	**51%**
▬▬▬▬▬▬▬▬▬	**50%**
▬▬▬▬▬▬▬▬▬▬▬	**63%**

n=U.S. engaged churchgoing Christians: 1,500 adults 35 and older, 856 adults 18 to 34, 464 teens 13 to 17, Dec. 2018–Jan. 2019.

What Is the Right Balance Between Aid & Evangelism?

Some Christians' reluctance to talk about missions, evangelism and other "churchy stuff" reflects inner questioning about their value. Our home culture in the U.S. is a pluralistic society that makes deliberate space for all kinds of religious beliefs and faith practices. What does that mean for sharing faith with non-Christians? Do engaged Protestant Christians believe the Great Commission is for them, here in their everyday American lives?[*]

In large measure, yes. A majority of teens, young adults and older adults agrees that "what Jesus told his disciples—'Go and make disciples of all nations'—applies to me." Most are convinced (even if they don't like the language of "conversion" or "winning souls") that disciple-making is a calling on all of Christ's followers.

That said, it's helpful to note where there is softening of this conviction: among supportive skeptics across all ages. Most of this group still

[*] Do they even know what it is? As Barna found in *Translating the Great Commission* (2018), half of practicing Christians don't recognize the term (51%).

CHAPTER

4

owns the Great Commission to some extent—but, as we have seen elsewhere, many also have qualms about why, when and how it's carried out.

Young adults who are otherwise engaged in their faith but do not regularly attend church are more likely than churchgoers to *disagree* that the Great Commission applies to them (20% vs. 9%).

Among engaged Christian young adults who are *not* convinced about the Great Commission's personal applicability, there is lower overall missions engagement. For instance, they are much less likely than those who *do* take gospel-sharing responsibility to say giving to missions (44% vs. 58%), praying for missionaries (38% vs. 59%), going on a short-term mission (25% vs. 44%) or even learning about other

"What Jesus Told His Disciples—
'Go and Make Disciples of All Nations'—Applies to Me"

● Agree strongly ● Agree somewhat

	Agree strongly	Agree somewhat
Teens 13–17	54%	37%
Young adults 18–34	58%	33%
Older adults 35+	59%	34%

n=U.S. engaged churchgoing Christians: 1,500 adults 35 and older, 856 adults 18 to 34, 464 teens 13 to 17, Dec. 2018–Jan. 2019.

Supportive Skeptics: **"What Jesus Told His Disciples—**
'Go and Make Disciples of All Nations'—Applies to Me"

● Agree strongly ● Agree somewhat

	Agree strongly	Agree somewhat
Teens 13–17	38%	49%
Young adults 18–34	40%	48%
Older adults 35+	39%	49%

n=U.S. engaged churchgoing Christian supportive skeptics: 306 adults 35 and older, 228 adults 18 to 34, 99 teens 13 to 17, Dec. 2018–Jan. 2019.

cultures (41% vs. 57%) is likely to be in their future. So this lack of personal responsibility doesn't just impact direct gospel-sharing activities; for some Christians, it correlates with a collapse of their missional drive.

Cross-Cultural Evangelism

Sharing the gospel across cultures adds layers of complexity to questions surrounding evangelism. Missiologists—practical theologians

Evolving Over the Long Haul

Donna & Jim are Canadians who have served in East Africa for more than 30 years. Donna grew up on the mission field, met Jim at college back in Canada and then finished her nurse-midwife training in Uganda. She has served in various roles related to women's health, including midwifery care, nurse training and facility administration. Jim is an educator, starting with teaching English literature to missionary kids in Kenya and most recently sustainable agriculture for farming families near Arusha, Tanzania.

In their view, pre-1990s missions to Africa was almost exclusively focused on evangelism and church planting. Their vocations—women's health (Donna) and education (Jim)—began as side hustles in service to this "more important" missions calling. Over time, however, their side hustles have taken center stage. They view their work as Kingdom-centered, God-glorifying and good in and of itself, and look for opportunities to share the gospel in Tanzania just as they do when back in Canada: in and through their everyday relationships.

Looking forward, Donna and Jim see the Church's center of gravity shifting to the global South. They believe the Church in East Africa is on the cusp of exponential growth, which will include sending missionaries throughout the world. "The Church is the world's most diverse organization," Jim says, and a healthy future for global missions will lean into this diversity.

A lack of personal responsibility regarding the Great Commission doesn't only impact gospel-sharing activities; for some, it correlates with a collapse of missional drive

who investigate the Church's mission—have been thinking and writing about this complexity for many years, long before the modern era of globalization and pluralism. Jesuit Matteo Ricci, for example, reintroduced Christianity to China in the 17th century by adapting the faith to the Chinese worldview, even permitting ancestor veneration as part of Catholic practice.[8] This adaptation process later became known as "inculturation," whereby Christian theology and practices are contextualized for different cultures.[9]

More recently, Lesslie Newbigin was a British missionary to India beginning in the 1930s whose reflections on the impact of history (especially Western history) on the Church's overall mission project have become modern classics of missiological thought.[10] Most mission-sending agencies have changed their views of and approaches to cross-cultural ministry, informed by Newbigin and other missiologists. For example, many Christians still admire Jim Elliot, one of the American evangelists killed in 1956 by an uncontacted tribe in Ecuador, but few of today's missionaries adopt his methods—and most would criticize the few who do.* Cross-cultural evangelism has changed. By and large, faith-sharing missionaries today seek to "evangelize, not Westernize," and undergo rigorous training on how to share good news about Jesus in culturally sensitive ways.

Not all engaged Christians know about these changes, and even those who do may feel hesitant about cross-cultural faith sharing. Analysts looked again at some of the "missionaries should" statements and divided them into two categories: *aid* and *evangelism*. Doing so enabled researchers to observe engaged Christians' preferences, if any, for one over the other. What they found is a plurality of young adults (43%), older adults (45%) and teens (45%) who express a desire for both. A smaller but significant percentage in each age cohort prefers that evangelism be given priority (34% teens, 32% young adults, 35% adults 35+).

*A recent example is the mixed response from the missions community to John Allen Chau's death in 2018.

Supportive Skeptics Are More Likely to Prefer Aid Over Evangelism

● Aid over evangelism   ● Evangelism over aid   ● Both   ● No preference

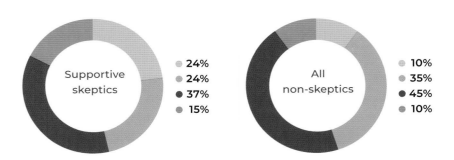

Supportive skeptics		All non-skeptics	
● 24%		● 10%	
● 24%		● 35%	
● 37%		● 45%	
● 15%		● 10%	

n=856 U.S. engaged churchgoing Christians 18 to 34, Dec. 2018–Jan. 2019.

What Responsibilities Do Missionaries Have to You, as a Financial Supporter?

% "agree"

● "to make new Christians"   ● "to disciple Christians effectively"   ● "to save lives"

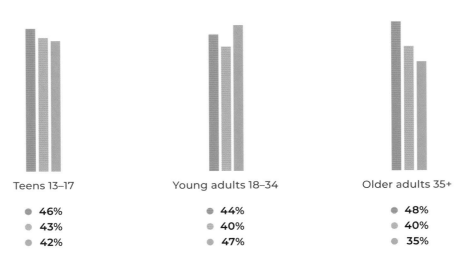

Teens 13–17	Young adults 18–34	Older adults 35+
● 46%	● 44%	● 48%
● 43%	● 40%	● 40%
● 42%	● 47%	● 35%

n=U.S. engaged churchgoing Christians: 1,500 adults 35 and older, 856 adults 18 to 34, 464 teens 13 to 17, Dec. 2018–Jan. 2019.

For many young
Christians,
humanitarian work
is and must be an
essential aspect of
21st-century missions

Before surveys went into the field, the Barna team hypothesized that young adults, given their comparatively stronger support for justice and mercy ministries, might be more likely than older adults to prefer aid over evangelism—and, in fact, that is what the data show, albeit by narrow margins. (Teens are more likely to express no preference.) Taking a closer look at these aid-preferring young Christians, we find that many are the supportive skeptics we're getting to know.

Finally, researchers asked engaged Christians about what they would hope for or expect, if they were to give money to missions. Over and above evangelism (44%) and discipleship (40%) activities, the largest plurality of churchgoing young adults, nearly half (47%), says they want missionaries "to save lives."

Everybody loves a humanitarian—and for good reason! People who live in service to meeting others' needs, often at great cost to themselves, not only make life better for those who are less fortunate but also set a positive moral example for those who are more fortunate. The good life is not all about getting, they remind us.

For many engaged Christian young adults, humanitarian work is and must be an essential aspect of 21st-century missions—at least as and sometimes more important than sharing the gospel of Christ.

- As you read the missionary profiles included in this report, are there any themes that resonate with you? What kind of work fascinates, excites or most inspires you? Are there any profiles that put you off?

- Would you say you're more aid-focused, evangelism-focused or an even blend of both when it comes to supporting or engaging in missions work? If you're drawn to one more than the other, where do you think your bias comes from?

- How do you feel about Christians whose missions focus runs in the other direction? How would you talk to that person about mission priorities?

Who Are Potential Missionaries?

They may not currently be planning or preparing for overseas Kingdom work, but something in the hearts of the engaged Christians Barna calls "potential missionaries"* lights up when they imagine themselves on mission. Here are demographic breakdowns and faith practices among potential missionaries in each age group, along with their responses related to missionary engagement. Can you spot the potential missionaries in your community? Maybe all they need to take the next step is your encouragement.

Half of Engaged Christian Young Adults Are Potential Missionaries

- Teens 13–17
- Young adults 18–34
- Older adults 35+

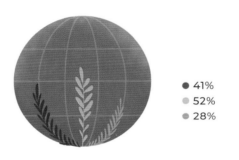

- 41%
- 52%
- 28%

Potential Missionaries Ages 18 to 34 Are More Open to Creative Mission Work Than Teens and Older Adults

% "definitely interested" among potential missionaries

- Teens 13–17
- Young adults 18–34
- Older adults 35+

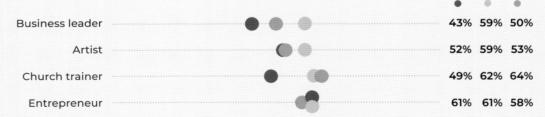

	Teens 13–17	Young adults 18–34	Older adults 35+
Business leader	43%	59%	50%
Artist	52%	59%	53%
Church trainer	49%	62%	64%
Entrepreneur	61%	61%	58%

*Potential missionaries are engaged Christians who say they are "definitely" interested in serving in one or more of the following missionary roles: business leader, artist, entrepreneur, church trainer.

● Potential missionaries ● All other engaged Christian young adults

...And They See Potential Everywhere

Young potential missionaries agree with other engaged Christians that missionaries should share God's love, help Christians better understand the faith and share the gospel. But differences emerge when we look at more practical or operational aspects of missions work—potential missionaries want missions to be all-of-the-above.

Their Exposure to Missions Yields Mission-Mindedness

Someone who has extensive experience with missions or who knows a missionary personally is more likely to be a potential missionary. This is not necessarily a cause-and-effect scenario, but there is a compelling argument here for the importance of early and often missions engagement.

% always should do

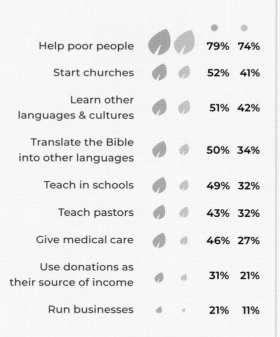

Help poor people	79%	74%
Start churches	52%	41%
Learn other languages & cultures	51%	42%
Translate the Bible into other languages	50%	34%
Teach in schools	49%	32%
Teach pastors	43%	32%
Give medical care	46%	27%
Use donations as their source of income	31%	21%
Run businesses	21%	11%

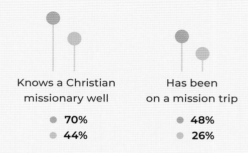

Knows a Christian missionary well
● 70%
● 44%

Has been on a mission trip
● 48%
● 26%

Longest mission trip

% among those who have been on a trip

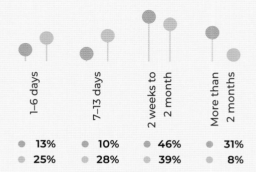

1–6 days	7–13 days	2 weeks to 2 month	More than 2 months
13%	10%	46%	31%
25%	28%	39%	8%

n=1,119 U.S. engaged Christians ages 18–34, Dec. 2018–Jan. 2019.

How Should
Missions Be Funded?

T he fundraising letter. It *looks* like a rare piece of hand-addressed personal mail with a stamp on it and everything, but then you tear it open and . . . well, the holy part of you wants to be fired up and supportive and moved by all God is doing around the world, and by your chance to participate in it.

And then there's the *other* part of you.

Among engaged Christians 35 and older who would change something about how missions work is done, one in four (26%) says missionaries need more support, financial and otherwise—the most common theme among older adults. By contrast, only a handful of younger Christians says this is what they would change. In fact, more young adults express money-related concerns in a different direction: skepticism about the fundraising model of supporting missions.

Researchers looked at engaged Christians' feelings about donation funding from several angles, trying to get a multi faceted view of this issue. For example, "use donations as their source of income"

Craftspeople Needed for Kingdom Building

Matt is a graphic designer and videographer who didn't know what to do with the sense that God was calling him to missions. Wasn't being a missionary just for preachers, teachers and doctors? Turns out, no. "Through Solomon, the Lord called craftsmen to build his temple, and they were just as important as the others who were part of it. Our role is to build God's Kingdom through creative work."

Using his skills, Matt helps fellow IMB missionaries tell their stories to supporters and donors. But he also offers his services to non-Christian NGOs, which has opened countless doors to share God's love with people who would otherwise never hear the gospel. "The door has never been as wide open as it is right now. There is so much opportunity for creative people, for creative entrepreneurs and craftsmen. There is so much need. We can connect with people that traditional pastors or church planters can't. We can bless communities and reach segments that others can't touch. To offer your abilities and art is a gift."

was included in the "missionaries do vs. should" series of statements. Engaged Christians of all ages have similar assessments of how often missionaries *do* this, but those under 35 are almost twice as likely as older Christians to judge that missionaries "never" *should* do this (27% young adults; 25% teens vs. 14% adults 35+).

Yet the vast majority of these same young Christians has personally made donations to missions. Nearly nine out of 10 (87%) have given money to a mission organization or directly to a missionary. (Unsurprisingly, since many missionaries primarily fundraise through local churches, regular church-going seems to influence this behavior: Young adults who have *not* attended a service in the past month are much less likely to have given to missions; 58%.) There seems to be a bit of a disconnect between young Christians' behavior (giving money to missions) and their feelings about that behavior. Again, we see many doing what they are "supposed" to do—engaging practically in the Church's mission—while dealing with ambivalence related to how that mission is carried out.

A few convey their ambivalence specifically about the donations model through their decision not to fundraise for their own mission endeavors. "I have done it and will never do it again," wrote one engaged Christian who has been on several short-term overseas trips. "If I can't fund it, it's not happening. It's not right to ask others to pay for my dreams; in my opinion, it cheapens the work."[11]

Others may have crowdfunding exhaustion, as donation-based giving sites such as GoFundMe, founded in 2010, have become more ubiquitous.

Still others are dealing with the economic reality common to many Millennials: student debt, lagging wages and a desire to spend limited discretionary income close to home. (Barna found in *The Generosity Gap* that Millennial practicing Christians prefer to give to people they personally know who have immediate needs.[12])

Whatever the case, a significant minority of young engaged Christians isn't sure that international missions is where their money can do the most good.

Planning to Give

Half of engaged churchgoing Christians 18 to 34 (53%) say they will definitely or probably give to a missions organization or a missionary in the next five years, only slightly less than the percentage of adults 35 and older who say so (57%). Non-churchgoers are far less likely to say they'll give to missions (30%).

Since we know supportive skeptics tend to be personally engaged in missions, it's not a surprise that they are just as likely, statistically speaking, as other engaged Christian young adults to say they'll give in the next five years (50% vs. 53%). As we've seen elsewhere, they are not interested in pulling the plug on their support—but that doesn't negate their concerns.

Christians under 35 are almost twice as likely as older believers to judge that missionaries should "never" use donations as their source of income

Young black
American Christians
are more likely
than young
white Christians to
express ambivalence
about the legacy
of Euro-American
missions

There is a group of engaged churchgoers, however, whose skepticism appears to impact the likelihood they will financially support mission endeavors: black Americans, across all age groups. As we saw in an earlier chapter, young black Christians, in particular, are more likely than young white Christians to express ambivalence about the legacy of Euro-American missions. That doubt may influence their decision making when it comes to donating resources to support future missions.

It might be that, as individual missionaries and sending organizations reckon with missions' past entanglement with colonialism and other injustices, black Americans will become more willing to lend their support, financial and otherwise. But it appears that, for now, many black Christians—especially young adults and teens—remain unconvinced.

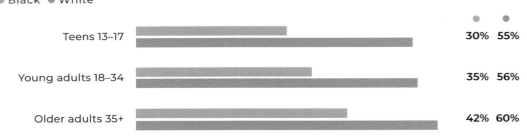

Ethnicity Correlates with Planning to Give to Missions

% "definitely + probably" in the next five years

● Black ● White

	Black	White
Teens 13–17	30%	55%
Young adults 18–34	35%	56%
Older adults 35+	42%	60%

n=U.S. engaged churchgoing Christians: 1,500 adults 35 and older, 856 adults 18 to 34, 464 teens 13 to 17, Dec. 2018–Jan. 2019.

- What feelings arose in you the last time someone asked for your financial support for missions? Try to discern how you felt about (1) the person who asked, (2) what kind of project they were raising money for and (3) the way they asked (e.g., GoFundMe or another crowdfunding platform, fundraising letter, face to face).

- If you're comfortable with the donations funding model of missionary support, what would you say to someone who isn't? If you have concerns about it, what are some alternatives?

- How should a young Christian personally prioritize missions giving? How should your local church? How can you help them both get their priorities straight?

What Should Accountability Look Like for Mission Work?

W e live in an era of diminishing trust in institutions, espe- cially among younger generations. During their lifetimes, Millennials have witnessed—and often borne the consequences of— massive failures in government, corporate, educational and religious institutions. As previous Barna studies have shown, many view those institutions and their leaders with understandable skepticism. (The "OK Boomer" meme of late 2019 was both a symptom and an outraged expression of this intergenerational skepticism.)

In addition to growing institutional distrust, there is widespread recognition that the internet, and especially social media, could offer opportunities for greater transparency and accountability. "Citizen journalism," wherein everyday people collect, record and report events and information, has democratized news to at least some extent and helped to create a cultural atmosphere that is hostile to closed-door meetings and backroom deal-making. Many people expect the sausage (so to speak) to be made in public.

Missionaries' Responsibilities to Their Financial Supporters

● Teens 13–17   ○ Young adults 18–34   ● Older adults 35+

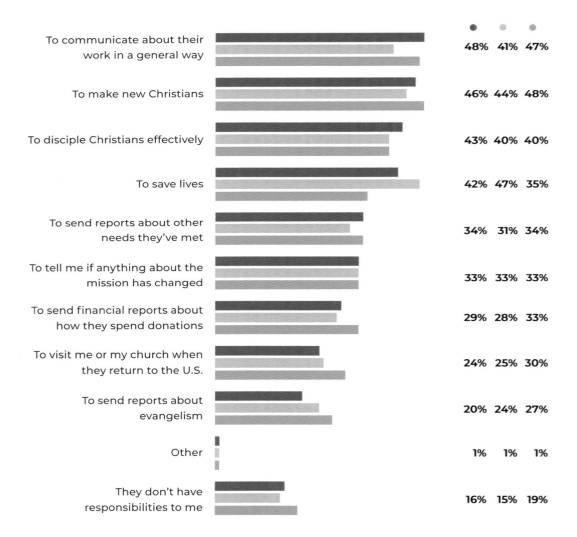

	●	●	●
To communicate about their work in a general way	48%	41%	47%
To make new Christians	46%	44%	48%
To disciple Christians effectively	43%	40%	40%
To save lives	42%	47%	35%
To send reports about other needs they've met	34%	31%	34%
To tell me if anything about the mission has changed	33%	33%	33%
To send financial reports about how they spend donations	29%	28%	33%
To visit me or my church when they return to the U.S.	24%	25%	30%
To send reports about evangelism	20%	24%	27%
Other	1%	1%	1%
They don't have responsibilities to me	16%	15%	19%

n=U.S. engaged churchgoing Christians: 1,500 adults 35 and older, 856 adults 18 to 34, 464 teens 13 to 17, Dec. 2018–Jan. 2019.

Given these realities and changing expectations, how do engaged Christians view accountability when it comes to missions? What do they expect from missionaries or missions organizations they support financially?

As we touched on briefly in chapter 4, "to save lives" is the top answer among young adults 18 to 34 (47%), beating out general

From Dental Hygiene to Soul Care

Jake is a dentist who felt called to missions from an early age. He very deliberately chose dentistry because he knew that skill set would allow him to serve in places that are closed to other types of Christian workers.

Ministering cross-culturally, he treats dental patients and trains community health workers in a remote area where a majority of people have yet to hear the good news. The country "has no dental school, no trained dentists, very little access to medical or dental care, so my work is about capacity building: Rather than operating a tradition-al clinic, I train national dental workers to do basic dental care. If they are followers of Jesus, I help train them to share their faith and make disciples. Our team also goes into villages to train families how to prevent and care for common illnesses."

Everyday life for his family can be a chal-lenge. "We're in a very isolated area, so at first it was, how do we find water every day? How do we get electricity? When our kids are sick, we don't have medical options. What do we do? How do we meet our basic needs? In all these things God has provided and been faithful.

"We have confidence that God will fin-ish the work he has begun here. This work is not an obligation, but an incredible gift. We get to partner with him to see his Kingdom come. Why would we consider doing some-thing else if *this* is an option? Why would I waste my life on something less important? Why *wouldn't* I want to invest my life in car-ing for the widow and the orphan? In loving my neighbor as myself and loving God with all my heart?"

communication (the most common answer among teens and older adults), evangelism and discipleship.

In general, men, regular churchgoers and black Americans are more concerned about some form of accountability, compared to women, non-churchgoers and people of other ethnicities (this holds true across age groups). For example, young women 18 to 34 (20%) are twice as likely as young men (9%) to say missionaries or organizations to whom they give money "don't have responsibilities to me."

As Barna has published elsewhere, 45 percent of U.S. adults say they would donate more toward global poverty if they knew the specific impact of their donation. This is most true of Millennials (62% vs. 32% of older generations). A "show your work" approach could also be helpful in retaining a majority of nonwhite Americans (57%) as donors (compared to 38% of white Americans).[13]

Interestingly, a strong correlate to high accountability expectations in this study is personally knowing a missionary. Among engaged Christian young adults, for instance, those who know a missionary well (58%) are higher on every accountability option than those who don't (42%). They want to know what's going on when it comes to their missions support.

Knowing a missionary has an impact on a variety of missionary engagement attitudes and behaviors—and always for the positive. For example, knowing a missionary makes a young Christian more likely to say that, in the next five years, they will give to missions (58% vs. 46% don't know a missionary), pray for missionaries (54% vs. 45%) and go on a short-term (40% vs. 30%) or long-term (22% vs. 9%) missions trip.

Why would this be?

Relationships matter. The influence of personal relationships on our opinions is called "contact effect," and it's a well-documented sociological phenomenon.[14]

Knowing a missionary has an impact on a variety of missionary engagement attitudes and behaviors—and always for the positive

Young Adults on Missionaries' Responsibilities to Their Financial Supporters, by Acquaintance with a Missionary

% among engaged Christian young adults

● Know missionary well ● Know missionary a little / not at all

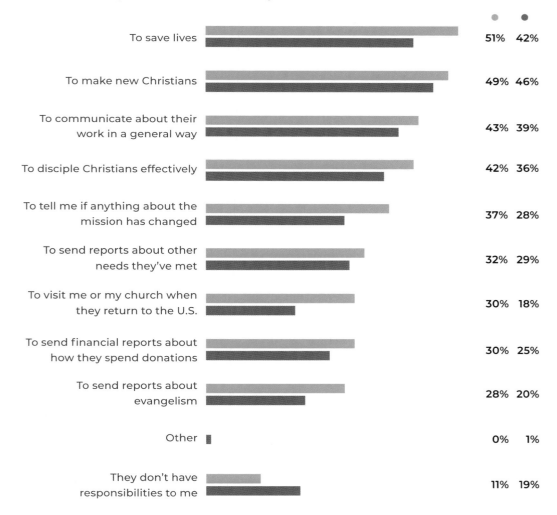

	Know missionary well	Know missionary a little / not at all
To save lives	51%	42%
To make new Christians	49%	46%
To communicate about their work in a general way	43%	39%
To disciple Christians effectively	42%	36%
To tell me if anything about the mission has changed	37%	28%
To send reports about other needs they've met	32%	29%
To visit me or my church when they return to the U.S.	30%	18%
To send financial reports about how they spend donations	30%	25%
To send reports about evangelism	28%	20%
Other	0%	1%
They don't have responsibilities to me	11%	19%

n=856 U.S. engaged churchgoing Christians 18 to 34, Dec. 2018–Jan. 2019.

Among institutionally skeptical younger generations, relationships *are* accountability

Here's a recent example from social science. Using the General Social Survey, a biannual national survey of opinions on a range of issues, Penn State sociologist Daniel DellaPosta was able to identify the evolution of people's attitudes toward homosexuality in tandem with the percentage of Americans who say they personally know an LGBT person.[15] Perhaps unsurprisingly, DellaPosta and his team found that knowing someone who identifies as LGBT increases one's likelihood of viewing homosexuality as morally acceptable.

Another example, this time from Barna: In 2016, one-quarter of U.S. adults who had spent time with a Muslim friend (24%) strongly disagreed that the majority of terrorism is perpetrated by Muslims, compared to 13 percent among those who had *not* spent time with a Muslim friend.[16] So friendship with a Muslim person plays a role in how this question is answered—hence, the contact effect.

The contact effect is alive and well when it comes to missions. Young engaged Christians who know a missionary well are more likely than those who don't to say the work missionaries do is "very valuable" (75% vs. 68%). But, similar to supportive skeptics (who, remember, aren't that confident about missions' value), their support tends to be qualified and informed. Specifically, they're more likely to strongly agree that mission work, if not done with proper caution, can lead to unhealthy dependence (16% vs. 7%); that, in the past, missions work has sometimes been unethical (16% vs. 8%); that charity work can hurt the local economy (13% vs. 6%); and that "Christianity should fix its reputation before doing more missions" (17% vs. 10%). (Supportive skeptics are similar in their responses to these statements.)

The takeaway here is that, among institutionally skeptical younger generations, relationships *are* accountability. Of course they are interested, just like older Christians, in the nuts and bolts of good fiscal management and responsible cross-cultural dealings. But all of that must be within the context of strong relationships with those whom they are sending on mission.

- Does good accountability for individual missionaries look different from good accountability for sending organizations? If not, why not? If so, how?

- What do you think about the idea that "relationship is accountability"? Is it enough when it comes to missions? If not, what kind of institutional checks are appropriate or necessary?

- In the conversation that follows this chapter, Erin and Julian Williams make a case that short-term missions should be suspended or discarded altogether. After reading their ideas, what do you think? Why?

Supportive Skeptics in Conversation

ERIN & JULIAN WILLIAMS

Erin: Here's something I think is going right with U.S.-based overseas missions: the turn toward meeting tangible needs, toward seeking justice and acting in mercy. If people are hungry, it's wrong to bring them only spiritual food if it's in our power to meet their physical need. It's not just impractical—I mean, it's absurd to expect people to care about what we have to say if we don't care about them first—but it also ignores Christ's calling on us to feed the hungry, clothe the naked, and so on. So I'm glad to see many organizations shifting their focus.

Julian: I feel encouraged by the deliberate effort to listen to and amplify the voices of people of color when it comes to missions. Missionaries, missions organizations and leaders of those organizations have been homogeneously white since forever, but I see a real effort to change that. It's seriously crazy to think that people from one cultural background, most of whom don't worship with black or brown people even in their home church, should launch themselves into a world full of black and brown and whatever-shade people without some significant cultural training. There seems to be a genuine effort, with the help and leadership of people of color, to count the cost of that approach and to change.

Which brings me to something that, in my view, is going wrong with missions. I think the missions establishment, the "missions machine," when I'm feeling cynical, has to count the cost of short-term trips. Sending young people to serve cross-culturally is a costly shortcut for forming them into members of Christ's multicultural Body. It's not a cost worth paying, and I say that as somebody who wouldn't be who I am without short-term missions experiences.

Erin: Same for me. I think about my training in mental health and I can barely stand to consider the countless kids who have been left more emotionally impoverished because of so many people coming and going, holding them close for a couple of days or weeks and then gone forever. In trying to do good, what damage have we done? We have to reckon with the unintended but real and lasting consequences of how we do missions.

Julian: It's not up to poor children in developing countries to teach our privileged kids how blessed they are. Those children are *children*.

ERIN WILLIAMS spent 10 years in church ministry, international missions and leadership development, and then earned a master's degree in marriage and family therapy from Nyack College. She now practices as a marriage and family therapist at a faith-based private practice in Atlanta. Williams has a passion to integrate spiritual and emotional health by providing safe spaces for people of every identity, background, race or gender to experience the fullness of their God-given identity.

JULIAN WILLIAMS holds a master's degree in intercultural studies from Nyack College and a bachelor's in organizational development from Pepperdine University. His dream is to motivate people in our culture and others toward personal, professional and spiritual development in an increasingly dynamic world of service and pioneering. He lives in Atlanta and serves as the founder of BlueSalt Recruiting & Development.

Erin and Julian met while serving with an organization that sends short-term missionaries around the world. They credit their missions experiences with helping to form their priorities and identities.

Our kids are not their job. If we want our kids to be culturally well-rounded, that's up to us. Plus, if we truly want to help poor children in developing countries, are *our kids* the best people to do it? Come on, no.

On top of all that, are short-term trips really as life-changing as we think? The course of *our* lives and ministry changed because of missions, absolutely. But I can think of dozens of people we served with for whom that wasn't the case, and half a dozen more who walked away from faith and church *because of* their missions experience. It just wrecked them. Erin and I are more the exception than the rule.

Erin: And even the real good that has come and is coming of our missions experiences is, I think, more a result of God's redemption than an outcome of the experiences in and of themselves. God is using and redeeming our missions involvement in profound and powerful ways, but that doesn't mean nothing needs to change. Just because I got something out of it doesn't make it an unvarnished good.

As far as I'm concerned, the burden of proof is on people who say short-term missions is good. Just because we've been doing it this way for years and years doesn't mean we should keep doing it.

Julian: Like so much having to do with faith, wrestling with these questions isn't optional. It's awkward and difficult and uncomfortable, but the life of faith isn't about comfort anyway—the opposite, really. So often, following Jesus is about getting outside of what makes us comfortable socially, economically, relationally. I think there's a sense in which going to serve far away can be more comfortable, or at least less uncomfortable, than serving close to home. Families will send their kids to all the crazy war-torn or poverty-stricken places around the world but won't go with them to the poor and violent neighborhoods of their own city. It would be laughable if it didn't make me so angry.

We can't "drop off" the gospel, whether we're close to home or far away. The gospel is not delivered, it's lived. Incarnated. The way we do missions has to embody the truth of incarnation, and I don't think the short-term model passes the smell test. Jesus has to be our model, our archetype for mission. He embodied our flesh to show us what God is like! He didn't stand outside human culture and mock it, laughing to his buddies about how superstitious we are and then demanding we abandon all our silly hocus pocus. He came *into* a human culture, became a part of it! He showed how the Father was already at work within that culture and sent his Spirit to renew and restore people *and* their culture. Are we really so arrogant to believe that God isn't already working in places we haven't been to? Like, he hasn't made the trip until we bring him along in our carry-on?

Erin: That mentality makes us the hero of the story, and it's toxic. We have to purge ourselves from the deception that we know best. That's not how relationships work! Of course we have a lot to offer, as comparatively rich Christians in the global North. God is working in our culture, too. But if we truly care about the gospel and the Church's mission, humility and teachability have to become the greater part of our posture. The Church is growing in the global South, and it's just possible that we have more to learn from them than they do from us.

The fact that these conversations are even happening gives me hope. God *is* at work. He's redeeming me, he's redeeming us and our missions experiences. And I have faith he'll continue working and redeeming in the future, in spite of us. But I don't want him to *have to* work in spite of me. I want to see the new thing God's Spirit is doing and get on board with that.

Is There a Place for a New Kind of Missionary?

A s we've seen in the profiles of missions workers throughout this report, some missionaries run businesses as part of their work. Whether it's tech investing in Asia or managing an art gallery in Berlin, these cross-cultural workers see their for-profit efforts as much more than making money.

The blending of business and social good has become culturally commonplace, even expected, especially among younger generations. For example, the "buy one, give one" model, pioneered by Toms Shoes, has been around for nearly 15 years—long enough for both the upsides and the downsides to surface. Accordingly, many young adults are aware of the pros *and* cons when it comes to mixing business and social causes.

Engaged Christians in the U.S. are divided in their opinions when it comes to whether missionaries *should* run businesses. Half of teens, young adults 18 to 34 and adults 35 and older are in agreement that missionaries should "sometimes" do so, but younger adults are more

If they want to garner young black support, missionaries need to be ready to explain exactly how and why they engage in business building

likely to have firmer opinions when it comes to "always" (16%) and especially "never" (19%), while teens (24%) and older adults (20%) are more comfortable saying "I don't know."

It's worth pointing out that, if younger Christians are skeptical about the donations model of missions support, then concurrently they *ought* to be more open to innovative approaches—like entrepreneurship—to sustain missionaries overseas. But, as is so often the case, there appears to be a lot of ambivalence and even cognitive dissonance when it comes to money issues.

Digging into the demographics, we find that young black engaged Christians are more polarized than whites on this question (this is often the case among black Americans). One-quarter says missionaries should "never" run businesses (25% vs. 17% white young adults) and

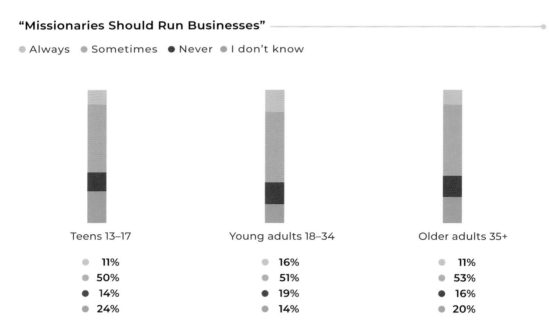

"Missionaries Should Run Businesses"

● Always ● Sometimes ● Never ● I don't know

Teens 13–17	Young adults 18–34	Older adults 35+
● 11%	● 16%	● 11%
● 50%	● 51%	● 53%
● 14%	● 19%	● 16%
● 24%	● 14%	● 20%

n=U.S. engaged churchgoing Christians: 1,500 adults 35 and older, 856 adults 18 to 34, 464 teens 13 to 17, Dec. 2018–Jan. 2019.

one-third says they "always" should do so (33% vs. 13%). It's unclear exactly what factors are at work here, but enthusiasm for economic empowerment and concerns about worker exploitation (for example) are not mutually exclusive. If they want to garner young black support, sending organizations and missionaries alike need to be ready to explain exactly how and why they engage in business building.

Missional Businesspeople

Hearing from people on the mission field over the past decade or so, Barna found strong evidence that the roles of missionaries have evolved and expanded. In particular, many incorporate marketplace work alongside their ministry.

There are myriad examples, but here are a few:

- A team of doctors in an area of Peru where there is extreme wealth inequality came up with the idea of a tiered payment system for medical care. The handful of very wealthy residents are willing to pay well for high-quality care, which means the doctors can offer low- or no-cost

The Art of Living Like Jesus

MaryJo is an artist who lives, paints and runs a gallery in Berlin. She views her calling through the eyes of an artist. "Coming to follow Christ is a lot like art: It's a process. So missions is more than evangelism, telling people to repent and believe in Jesus, getting them to say a prayer or whatever. I mean, look at the way Jesus himself did life and ministry! He was genuinely interested in people and their needs. He ate with them, got to know them.

"That's all I do, try to follow Christ's example . . . but as an artist, not a preacher. Whether it's hosting a potluck, sharing ideas about technique with a young painter or telling my own faith story, it's all mission."

Transferred for the Sake of the Gospel

Sensing God's call to Southeast Asia, Greg submitted a request to be transferred to a large city where the multinational company for which he works has an office. He and his wife, Lily, relocated with their four children as self-supported missionary associates with IMB.

Lily volunteers in a pregnancy care clinic that ministers to refugee women, and leads a Bible study through which several Central Asian women who serve as translators at the clinic have come to faith in Jesus.

Greg leads a large team just as he did in the States, only now he has a chance to encourage the small number of Christians on his staff and equip them for discipleship. He offers after-hours seeker-friendly Bible studies that are open to anyone. He says, "There are such incredible things going on in the world, among English being so widely spoken, and easy airline travel, and the internet and multinational corporations. It's a special, unique time in history to reach the nations."

care to the poorest residents. The same team purchased LASIK equipment for correcting vision problems. When they are not using it, they rent it out to other providers and then use the funds to support an orphanage in their community.

- A tech developer started an innovation hub in a major African city where he offers training, mentorship and networking to young aspiring tech entrepreneurs, as well as Bible and discipleship classes during off-hours.

- An anthropologist in rural Cambodia is using her international connections to open new markets for local artisans, enabling them to sell their work to collectors around the world.

To learn whether non-traditional mission initiatives are an appealing path for young adults, the research team provided composite profiles of different missionaries—an entrepreneur, business leader, artist and church trainer—and asked participants to indicate their interest.

Here are the two business-focused descriptions:

BUSINESS LEADER

Upon graduating from college with an economics degree, Amanda went to work for a "Big Four" accounting firm. After a few years of developing her skills, she had an opportunity to transfer to one of the firm's global offices in Southeast Asia, and thought it would be a great adventure to live overseas. Amanda connected with a missions agency to explore how she might be intentional about sharing her faith with the people in her new community—both at work and in her neighborhood—who had never been introduced to the Bible or Jesus. Amanda is progressing in her career, working full time, while also living life on-mission in Southeast Asia.

ENTREPRENEUR

An entrepreneur at heart, Matt had led a couple of start-up ventures during and after college, but he longed to build a company that would make a "God-sized" impact. A college friend who came to the U.S. from a region that was "closed" to Christianity talked about opportunities for economic development in his home country, and Matt began to dream big. What if he could start a business in that country, which would provide both jobs that would help the local population economically as well as open doors to engage people with the gospel? He found an agency that specialized in "business as mission" and went through training to prepare for this new opportunity. They provided organizational and economic counsel, cross-cultural training and advice on how to engage employees of the new company—for example, on-the-job conversations or after-hours Bible studies where employees would face less interrogation from friends and family than if they attempted to attend a Christian gathering elsewhere. Two years in, Matt's business is growing, the local community is changing and people who never heard of Jesus are coming to faith. Matt says this is the best dividend any entrepreneur could enjoy.

Teens, young adults and older adults were asked to read the descriptions and then evaluate, first, if they would consider taking such a missionary role themselves and, second, if they would financially support a missionary like the fictional composite. Young adults 18 to 34 are much more likely than teens and older adults to respond in the affirmative across the board. There is significant enthusiasm among Millennial engaged Christians for these nontraditional missionary roles.

Arts on Mission

What about other innovative forms of mission work? According to Andrew Shaughnessey at Mission to the World, "We have artists in Japan and Australia, the South Pacific and a couple of places in Europe.

Interest in Becoming or Supporting This Kind of Missionary:
Business Leader & Entrepreneur

% "definitely"

- Become a business leader
- Support a business leader
- Become an entrepreneur
- Support an entrepreneur

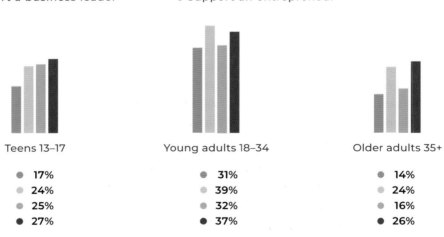

Teens 13–17	Young adults 18–34	Older adults 35+
● 17%	● 31%	● 14%
● 24%	● 39%	● 24%
● 25%	● 32%	● 16%
● 27%	● 37%	● 26%

n=U.S. engaged churchgoing Christians: 1,500 adults 35 and older, 856 adults 18 to 34, 464 teens 13 to 17, Dec. 2018–Jan. 2019.

Art is a way people connect with each other and with God, so there's a natural affinity with missions."

ARTIST

Kayla was always interested in fine arts and studied under some great teachers in her college years. She was also committed to her faith and considered going into ministry or serving as a missionary in another country for a time, but she was reluctant to hang up her artistic gifts. After connecting with another Christian artist on a trip to Europe, Kayla realized the opportunity to combine her passions. A missions agency helped her join an art community in a secular European city, where she could work side by side with other artists, stretching her skills in new directions, and also form relationships with locals to begin to open doors to share about her faith. Kayla now calls this European city her home and manages a gallery and studio where she holds community workshops and collaborates with other artists and is, little by little, bringing the hope of the gospel to a post-Christian culture.

Again (see p. 72) we see outsized interest among adults 18 to 34 compared to teens and older adults. Interest in personally taking this kind of role is highest among black Americans (40% vs. 30% all others).

Empowering Local Christian Leaders

The church trainer is the most traditional of the missionary profiles tested in the survey, and it's where we clearly see the type of response we would expect from those who are most ambivalent about missions—that is, the supportive skeptics.

CHURCH TRAINER

Aaron always knew he wanted to be in ministry and figured his best option to make an impact would be in a local church where he could get to know the people well and build deep relationships. He enrolled in seminary to prepare

"Art is a way people connect with each other and with God, so there's a natural affinity with missions"

for ministry and interned at a church in the area. But after a time, God put on his heart a burden for the lost in other countries as well, and he began to explore some options. A door opened to move overseas to be a trainer for church leaders in a country where only a tiny minority of the population is Christian. On a visit, he saw how people were being introduced to the Bible in rural villages, becoming Christians and then starting their own churches because none existed where they lived. Soon they were church leaders in their community, inspiring other new Christians to also pursue ministry, but none of them had any formal theological training. Aaron was placed as a teacher and trainer to help these young leaders develop deeper knowledge of the Bible and skills to start and develop churches in their region. The relationships he developed with these young Christians, and the encouragement of seeing

Interest in Becoming or Supporting This Kind of Missionary: Artist & Church Trainer

% "definitely"

- Become an artist
- Support an artist
- Become a church trainer
- Support a church trainer

Teens 13–17	Young adults 18–34	Older adults 35+
21%	30%	15%
26%	37%	23%
20%	32%	18%
31%	45%	36%

n=U.S. engaged churchgoing Christians: 1,500 adults 35 and older, 856 adults 18 to 34, 464 teens 13 to 17, Dec. 2018–Jan. 2019.

their faith in action, still inspire him today as he serves in the field as a church-leader trainer.

Supportive skeptics 18 to 34 diverge most decisively from other young engaged Christians when it comes to financial support: Just about one-third (37%) says they would "definitely" donate to a church trainer like Aaron, compared to nearly half of others (47%).

So this type of missionary role garners the highest level of support, compared to the other roles (artist, entrepreneur, etc.), among those who are *not* skeptical about missions. There is clearly an appetite among these young, less-skeptical Christians for a more traditional, more direct approach to mission.

MISSIONS & YOU

- When you think of the word "missionary," is there a particular job function or set of skills that come to mind? What does "being a missionary" mean?

- As you read the four composite profiles, are there one or two that personally resonate with you? Would you want to support that kind of missionary or be that kind of missionary? Is there someone in your church or wider sphere of influence who comes to mind as a good fit for one or more of the four profiles?

- Do you *not* like any of the four profiles? Why? What are your concerns?

Who Are the Young Christians Who See Themselves on Mission?

As we saw in the previous chapter, there is considerable interest, especially among engaged Christians 18 to 34, in four missionary roles that are quite different from the culturally insensitive evangelist stereotype that many find objectionable. Researchers were eager to drill down on this interest, so they clustered those who say they would "definitely" consider taking at least one of the roles—business leader, entrepreneur, artist, church trainer—into a group called "potential missionaries." Young adults 18 to 34 are far more likely than teens and older adults to be potential missionaries. (See p. 76.)

The findings are stunning: *Half* of engaged churchgoing young adults are open to God's call to serve overseas! Are they currently planning on it? Based on their answers to the question about what kinds of missions engagement are likely for them, no: Just one in six young adults (17%) says long-term missions and one in three (36%) says short-term missions will be in their future (still, higher percentages than among older adults).

% who would "definitely" be interested in serving in one or more missionary roles

● Teens 13–17   ● Young adults 18–34   ● Older adults 35+

● **41%**
● **52%**
● **28%**

n=U.S. engaged churchgoing Christians: 1,500 adults 35 and older, 856 adults 18 to 34, 464 teens 13 to 17, Dec. 2018–Jan. 2019.

Even so, when given a chance to imagine themselves serving in specific missionary roles, half of engaged 18–34-year-olds say yes, they can see it. Let's meet them.

Researchers were surprised at first that a significantly larger proportion of young men (58% of all engaged churchgoing men 18 to 34) than young women (45%) qualifies as potential missionaries. Male self-identified Christians of any generation have long been less likely than their female counterparts to engage in faith-related activities like weekly Bible reading (33% men vs. 37% women) and prayer (65% vs. 73%), so the high level of engagement among the engaged Christian young men in this study was, in the early days of analysis, unexpected. These young men are more likely than young women to say that, in the past seven days, they have read the Bible on their own (84% vs. 77% women), attended a small group or Bible study (62% vs. 53%) and volunteered at church (58% vs. 45%). By their own accounts, they are deeply invested in their own faith and in the life of their church community.

The more the Barna team wrestled with these numbers, young men's rock-solid commitment (and women's hesitation) began to

> Given a chance to imagine themselves serving in specific missionary roles, half of engaged 18–34-year-olds say yes, they can see it

Continued on page 80.

Opening Doors Out of Sex Work

Rachel and her husband, Kyle, felt a specific calling to Berlin, and were sent as missionaries in the mid-2000s without a definite plan for their work. The city, like most of Western Europe, is highly post-Christian, and their sending organization knew that tried-and-true "unreached people" outreach methods would not likely bear much fruit. But Rachel and Kyle believed that an emphasis on listening, hospitality and prayer could help them discern how to offer good news to Berliners in ways they could receive, and the sending organziation prayerfully took a chance on their open-ended calling.

One of the places Rachel listened was in a café run by Christians in Kurfürstenstrasse, Berlin's unofficial red-light district, where she worked for eight years. One of the laments she heard again and again from women who wanted to leave prostitution was about their lack of options. They had nowhere to go, few job alternatives and many didn't even speak German. (Sex trafficking from Eastern Europe, Asia and North Africa is quite common.) "I thought God was directing me to open a recovery and transition safehouse for the sexually exploited—but I wanted to be sure, so I asked him for a clear sign. After about a year of prayer, I was in Atlanta to meet with the head of our denomination and tell him about the idea. On my way to the meeting, a homeless man walked up to me and said, 'You want to open a women's house. God says to trust him.' So . . ." Rachel laughs, "that's what I did.

"We don't focus on evangelism. There isn't enough trust, and there's too much trauma. They've been oppressed and forced and, understandably, they don't want any more pressure. They know we're Christians and that we pray for them. We show God by sharing love, respect, dignity, patience, kindness and perseverance. We don't judge and we don't give up.

"People have lots of theories about ministry to people who have been trafficked. They get all fired up about social justice. But the reality is very different. It's exhausting and easy to get discouraged mentally, physically and spiritually. You have to deal with your own brokenness and trauma."

And, Rachel says, she wouldn't have it any other way.

The Future of Missions Depends on Dealing with the Past

Young Engaged Christians, Especially Black Churchgoers, Are Eager to Engage with Missions

Black, Hispanic and other young people of color are more likely than their white counterparts to be potential missionaries and to say they will financially support a missionary. This is good news, since younger generations are increasingly diverse and missions belongs to the whole Church.

● Black   ● White   ● Hispanic   ● All ethnic minorities

% potential missionaries   *% will support a missionary*

% potential missionaries	% will support a missionary
● 61%	● 65%
● 48%	● 58%
● 54%	● 60%
● 57%	● 61%

...But They Also Have Reservations About the Past

Churchgoing Christians ages 18 to 34 are generally more concerned than older engaged believers with negative fallout from missions in the past—and concern is even greater among young black Americans. Yet, as we see on the previous page, young black Christians are more likely than young white Christians to express interest in future missions initiatives. **How can churches make space for these young leaders to help us deal well with the past and future?**

● Black   ● White   ● Hispanic   ● All ethnic minorities

"In the past, missions work has been unethical."
% agree

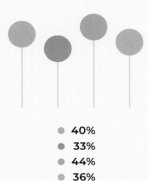

● 40%
● 33%
● 44%
● 36%

"Christian mission is tainted by its association with colonialism."
% agree

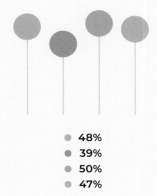

● 48%
● 39%
● 50%
● 47%

make sense. First, when it comes to men, as the cultural influence of Christianity diminishes, those who continue in pursuit of Christ—perhaps especially those who are male—tend to mean it. They are Christian *on purpose*, not by default, which means they prioritize and invest in practices like prayer, Bible reading, community and serving others that are essential to Christian life.

And, it seems, six in 10 of them (58%)—along with nearly half of engaged churchgoing young women (45%)—are ready to consider overseas ministry in some capacity.

Second, with regard to young women's comparative hesitancy, it's worth pointing out that they often have more to fear than men in terms of physical safety (this is true even at home, let alone in a foreign culture). And if they are in denominational traditions where fewer leadership opportunities are open to them based on their gender, they may not see the possibilities as easily as their male contemporaries.

Given the comparatively tepid feelings expressed by some black Americans toward missions, researchers were also somewhat surprised that, proportionally speaking, black engaged Christians 18 to 34 (61%) are more likely than white young adults (48%) to be potential missionaries. Remember, this means they would "definitely" consider at least one of the four roles included in the survey. Directionally, at least, black young adults are more likely than whites to say they would definitely consider taking *any* of the roles: artist (40% vs. 29%), entrepreneur (38% vs. 30% white), church trainer (39% vs. 30%) and business leader (35% vs. 27%).

Factors that did *not* come as a surprise involve other types of engagement; that is, someone's engagement in missions *at all* increases the chance they qualify as a potential missionary. The contact effect works in missions, too! For example, knowing a missionary well (63% vs. 36% of those who don't), having been on a previous missionary trip (67% vs. 43% of those who have not) and being a missionary kid (79% vs.

A person's engagement in missions *at all* increases the chance they qualify as a potential missionary

Young Adults on What Might Make Them More Likely to Go

● Potential missionaries ● All other engaged Christian young adults

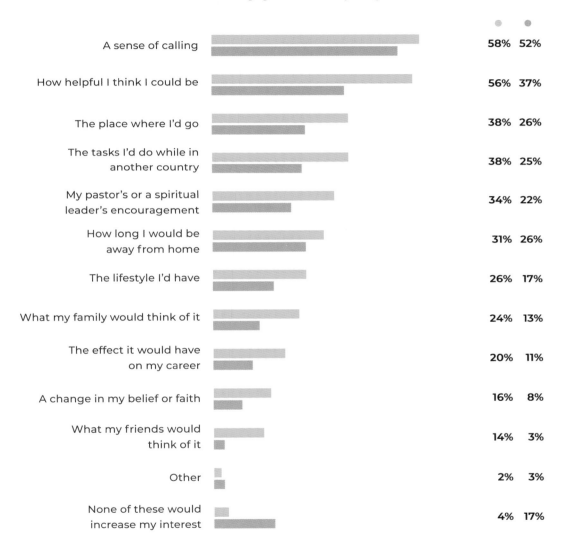

	●	●
A sense of calling	58%	52%
How helpful I think I could be	56%	37%
The place where I'd go	38%	26%
The tasks I'd do while in another country	38%	25%
My pastor's or a spiritual leader's encouragement	34%	22%
How long I would be away from home	31%	26%
The lifestyle I'd have	26%	17%
What my family would think of it	24%	13%
The effect it would have on my career	20%	11%
A change in my belief or faith	16%	8%
What my friends would think of it	14%	3%
Other	2%	3%
None of these would increase my interest	4%	17%

n=856 U.S. engaged churchgoing Christians ages 18 to 34, Dec. 2018–Jan. 2019.

49% of non-MKs) are all correlated with missionary potential. Also unsurprising is that engaged churchgoers who personally embrace the Great Commission ("What Jesus told his disciples applies to me") are more likely than those who don't to be potential missionaries (57% vs. 44%).

What Would Make Them More Likely to Go?

All young adults and teens were asked what, if anything, might increase their interest in going to another country as a missionary. There are not many significant differences between the two age groups, but when we compare potential missionaries 18 to 34 with those who don't qualify under the definition, we find that, in addition to a sense of calling, potential missionaries want to know that their work would make a difference. More than half say knowing "how helpful I could be" could elevate their personal interest in missions, confirming an earlier, similar Barna finding that people are more likely to get involved specifically in the fight against global poverty when they know they can make a difference.[17]

Could this be one key to nudging potential missionaries onto the field?

- Who are the potential missionaries among the Christian young adults and teens in your community or network? What kind of encouragement do they need to discern God's calling for their life? What's stopping you from offering that nudge?

- Who are the young women or African Americans that need you to open a door into missions or other ministry? What can you do to help?

- Previous Barna data, especially the findings for Kinnaman's book *Faith for Exiles*, suggest that young men need to be challenged toward more resilient faith. What can you do to help?

Everyday Life on Mission

Q&A WITH KAREN HUBER, GREATER MISSION EUROPE (IRELAND)

Q You've written elsewhere about being "on mission" as a family. That's a pretty big shift from just a few decades ago, when missionary kids (and sometimes missionary wives!) were, if not extraneous, then often peripheral to the missionary's calling. What does this posture mean for you and your family? Why is it important?

A Any missionary or full-time minister is aware of heroic missionary stories where the husband goes off pioneering, the wife cares for and educates the children, maybe he dies a martyr or she dies from going crazy due to isolation and abandonment. These true stories were elevated to us from ministry professors early on in our Bible college education! Before I had any clear calling to be a pastor or missionary's wife, that valorized imbalance in home and work, marriage and ministry, felt disingenuous at best and fatal at worst. It also created a mini-American Christian microculture that would be impossible for national believers to reproduce.

When we first arrived on the field, our older children were only five and two, and I soon became pregnant with our third. Though we planned and trained to be a "missionary family," I quickly realized I wasn't unlike those early missionary wives. It felt nearly impossible to fulfill a formal missionary role while caring for young kids, and I struggled with that tension.

KAREN HUBER is a writer whose work centers on culture, faith and parenting abroad. Originally from Kansas, Huber, her husband and three children serve with Greater Europe Mission in Dublin, Ireland, where they focus on discipleship, arts ministry and community restoration both within and outside the walls of the local church. Huber serves as an immigration and enculturation consultant for new cross-cultural workers in Europe while completing a Master of Arts in Literatures of Engagement. Visit www.karenohuber.com to learn more.

As they grew a bit older, my time with them became less all-consuming and our personality as a family began to unfold. At that point my husband and I reaffirmed that we wanted our posture as missionaries to holistically and organically fit into our family life.

We spent quite a bit of time learning from nontraditional "missional" U.S. church planters, as well as the 3DM model pioneered by Mike and Sally Breen. This way of being on mission as a family together—ministering to people in our home and community, inviting others into a church space that looks and feels like family and serving and worshipping alongside our kids—suited who we already were. And we didn't think we could survive long term any other way.

Of course, in each family's life, you encounter different seasons. So our current "family on mission" season looks like being actively involved in our kids' schools, leading a part of a small group that hosts monthly family dinners, prioritizing ministries that create a healthy balance between family and work and leading lives following Christ that can be reproduced by any Christian believer or family, no matter where they live.

Q You seem to personally have gone through ebbs and flows in your enthusiasm for the label "missionary." Is that a fair assessment? In your experience with other missionaries, is that ebb and flow fairly common? How do you fit that varying rhythm into an overall sense of calling?

A The term "missionary" is truly a double-edged sword. On the one hand, our host culture has a tremendous legacy: St. Patrick was the first missionary to Ireland and responsible for planting a Church that not only sent out missionaries around the known world, but kept scriptures safe and the Church alive under persecution for hundreds of years. And yet, the term has a troubling historical reputation for colonial ignorance and even brutality. Secularists in Europe today have an acute suspicion of the word as a harbinger of scandalized Catholicism and politically compromised American evangelicalism. And I don't think they're wrong.

For years, my husband and I did not consider entering the mission field because we were not what we considered to be the typical missionary: the evangelist. He felt a very specific calling to pastoral ministry, while my sense of calling was more peripheral. I studied journalism and communications, believing I had practical skills to offer to support Kingdom work. Simply put, we didn't fit the profile of the aforementioned missionary hero.

Even as we found a sending organization

we loved and believed in, I cringed inwardly at the expectations of missionaries, from both inside and outside the Church. From the inside, we felt the burden of metrics and miraculous conversions. From the outside, we felt the questioning glances and outright rejections from people burned by people seemingly just like us. I felt like I could please neither, so I laid down the moniker and let my husband lean into it instead.

When my children were younger, I felt freer to let the terms go and hide behind motherhood. Now, as I increasingly venture into marginal spaces and ministries of my own, I'm reckoning with what being a missionary really is. Part of that reckoning is taking on the task of redefining the term, or deciding if it's even worth it. But I believe the future of the Church, particularly in the U.S., demands a reckoning and a redefining. We owe it to our future writers and teachers, artists and administrators, who have a story of faith to tell. I'm now viewing an embrace of the term *missionary* to be as much about investing in my life with Jesus with my national friends as it is to introduce our passport-country churches to a more holistic, textured, honest portrayal of the disciple, both at home and abroad.

Q How do you see your other callings—parent, writer—in relationship with the missions experience? Is there tension there? Inspiration?

A I still primarily view myself and my calling to be as a writer and a mother; these are the two things that I feel define me as the person God created me to be. Only in a healthy pursuit and practice of them—especially in relation to my work as a writer, editor or graphic designer (whatever role I'm filling that week!)—twinned with obedience and openness to where God is at work in and around me, will I have anything of value to give those around me. Being part of a local writing community and global network of religion writers has given me so many opportunities to share my life, my story and my faith, and to learn from others doing similar work.

There is a tension, to be sure, but I wonder if there shouldn't be. I am a complex person in a nontraditional career raising a family in a country not our own (even if I have a passport for it!). I don't think I'd have much to offer my neighbor if I weren't leaning into the beauties and the difficulties of the life God has placed before me. I have so much to learn about our host culture, the Church, God's work here and where I—or any of us!—fit. Part of the tension is embracing a hungry yet humble posture and then being willing to do something about it, even if doing something sometimes looks like sitting still.

Q What is the biggest change you observe between how missions was done 20 years ago and how you're doing it now? Looking ahead 20 years, what do you think will be most different from today?

A Twenty years ago I was hearing those old missionary hero stories and thinking to myself, *I could never do that. I'm too loud, too rebellious, not the quiet and gentle submissive type. God would never use me and sending organizations wouldn't want to.* So it's fair to say I didn't give the status of missions a lot of careful thought until we arrived on the field.

From my perspective after 15 years in missions, I believe we are better at organizational financial accountability, but struggle more with (wise) personal transparency. We are better at cross-agency partnerships and working under the lead of national partners, but struggle more with interpersonal dynamics and handling cultural expectations.

I believe the days of the heroic Western missionary martyr is over. If we look at the recent tragic example of John Chau, we can see how the American Church is truly reconsidering our ideas of missions, evangelism and proselytizing. In some ways, it feels like we're just starting to look more critically at systems of power and entitlement, at what it means to export our religions to other cultures and how that plays into racial, ethical and cultural dynamics. To the evangelical church, it may feel brand new. But I think other Christian traditions, and surely the global Church, have been asking these questions for decades.

In the next 20 years, I think we need to re-examine and perhaps reinvent the missionary model, not just for the sake of healthy retention of long-term workers, but also due to ever-tightening visa regulations, especially in relation to tentmaking. We need to continue to push the conversation on defining the role of the missionary in a way that abides by local laws, honors the culture and the national Church and is financially sustainable. Some days I'm afraid those three things won't go hand in hand. But to be Christ's disciples in the world, we have to at least try.

Why Are Parents Sometimes a Barrier to Missions Engagement?

When researchers began to analyze data from the first wave of surveys among teens and young adults, they noticed that a small but significant minority cites "what my family would think" as a factor that could increase (and, presumably, decrease) their interest in going overseas for missions work. One-quarter of engaged Christian teens (23%) and one in six young adults (18%) say their family is a consideration.

Thinking about Christian families brought to researchers' minds a study Barna conducted a few years ago among Christian parents of prospective college students. Data showed that, when it comes to selecting a college, all except a small percentage rank their child's potential career success over other priorities. Christian parents don't look very different from their non-Christian counterparts when it comes to hopes for their child's future.[18]

On top of these quantitative indicators, a few researchers heard anecdotally from young Christians that "my parents would never want

Christian parents don't look very different from their non-Christian counterparts when it comes to hopes for their child's future

me to be a missionary." Could that be true? How do Christian parents feel about the prospect of their child going overseas on mission?

So, of course, Barna asked.

The second wave of research was conducted among engaged Christian parents whose children are ages 13 to 25. More than one in three says they are "very" open to the idea of their child becoming an international missionary, whether as a career (35%) or for just one or two years (39%), with about the same percentages saying they are "somewhat" open. That leaves about one-quarter of engaged Christian parents who aren't ready to express their support.

Parents' Openness to Their Child Serving in Missions

● Very open to the idea   ● Somewhat open to the idea

Becoming an international
missionary as a career 35% 39%

Becoming an international
missionary for 1–2 years 39% 38%

n=504 U.S. engaged churchgoing Christian parents, Sept. 2019.

Parents on Their Child's Interest in Missions

● Yes, at least one has
   expressed interest

● No, we talked about it and
   they aren't interested

● We've never talked about it

● 34%
● 20%
● 47%

n=504 U.S. engaged churchgoing Christian parents, Sept. 2019.

Parent Perceptions of & Attitudes Toward Missions

● Agree strongly   ● Agree somewhat

	Agree strongly	Agree somewhat
I would be able to trust God to watch over my child if he / she chose to serve as a missionary in another country	61%	34%
When it comes to being a missionary, the positives outweigh the negatives	47%	43%
Being a career missionary would be a very hard life in most countries	33%	51%
It is particularly dangerous for a single woman to be a career missionary in a foreign country	31%	49%
If my son or daughter became an international missionary, I would be constantly worried	22%	41%
In most foreign countries it's just too dangerous to be a missionary these days	18%	48%
I'd rather my child get a well-paying job than be a career missionary	15%	32%
Most people who enter the mission field end up struggling financially	12%	44%
It's very difficult for missionaries to transition when they leave the mission field	11%	41%
Serving in the mission field for several years can hinder your career later	9%	22%
It's usually a waste of time to get a college degree if you plan to be a missionary	7%	11%

n=504 U.S. engaged churchgoing Christian parents, Sept. 2019.

Most parents
say they would
encourage their
child's missions
engagement, but
many also entertain
doubts that could
act as a barrier

Two out of five parents (42%) say they would "definitely" encourage their child to be an international missionary if such an interest were expressed. Broken down by age, parents of teenagers (ages 13 to 17) are more likely than parents of young adults to say they would definitely encourage their child to serve in missions (45% vs. 35%).

One in three (34%) says their child actually has expressed interest in working on the mission field, but about half (47%) say they've never talked about it.

Although most parents have a positive view of Christian missionaries (79%) and say they would encourage their child's missions engagement, other data reveal that many also entertain doubts that could potentially act as a barrier to their child's service. As the chart on page 89 shows, most say they could trust God's provision for and protection of their missionary child, yet two-thirds agree at least somewhat that they would be constantly worried if their child were a missionary. Fewer than half strongly agree that, when it comes to being a missionary, the positives outweigh the negatives.

In addition to concerns about their child's safety, fears about his or her livelihood and future after missions also surface among engaged Christian parents. About half agree that most people who enter the mission field end up struggling financially, that it's very difficult for missionaries to transition after they leave the mission field and that they'd rather their child get a well-paying job than become a career missionary.

Other reasons parents mention for *not* encouraging their child to pursue international missions include worries about terrorism (64%), their child's safety in general (64%), health risks (51%), political instability (45%) and not being able to see or visit them often (49%), among others.

And yet, three out of four engaged Christian parents (72%) also say they'd be more likely to encourage their child if they truly believed

God were calling them to the mission field (see chart on page 92). Some might lend more support if their child were working for or under the care of a strong and well-established missions agency, if they were very spiritually mature or if they had a reliable source of funding and did not have to raise their own support.

Christian leaders can help parents release their children to answer God's calling. Barna interviewed a small focus group of parents of overseas missionaries; here's what some said about the role played by church leaders in helping their child discern his or her calling, what they felt or struggled with at the time and how their church community helps to sustain and encourage them during their child's time on the field:

- "Our church's mission pastor saw something in our daughter and encouraged her to attend Urbana [Student Missions Conference, hosted annually by InterVarsity]. We supported her trip, and it was there she really felt God calling her overseas. We weren't surprised, but I did have worries about safety and reliable communication."

- "My prayer life certainly grew!"

Momming on the Mission Field

Greta and her husband and five children serve with IMB in Europe. Greta spends about 20 hours a week helping her husband manage their larger missionary team but, in her view, raising their children *is* her mission—and it's an open door for ministry to other moms. Her family is both a calling in and of itself *and* the primary way Greta answers another of her callings: to share God's story with displaced Muslim women. "Our kids are an integral part of everything I do," she says.

From her point of view, raising children on mission isn't terribly different from how it would be here at home. There's still the tricky logistics of getting the older ones to school and extracurricular activities, and making sure the younger ones are in bed for naptime. Sharing the load with other mothers—carpooling, afterschool care, taking turns with the babies so every mom gets a chance to run errands—helps to form community, where real friendships can develop and the good news can take root.

> "After he chose the organization he eventually deployed with, I was on a mission to learn everything I could about it—its history, the way missionaries raise support, how they are resourced while on the field, what kind of support system they have for medical,

Factors That Could Increase Parents' Support

% among engaged Christian parents of children 13 to 25

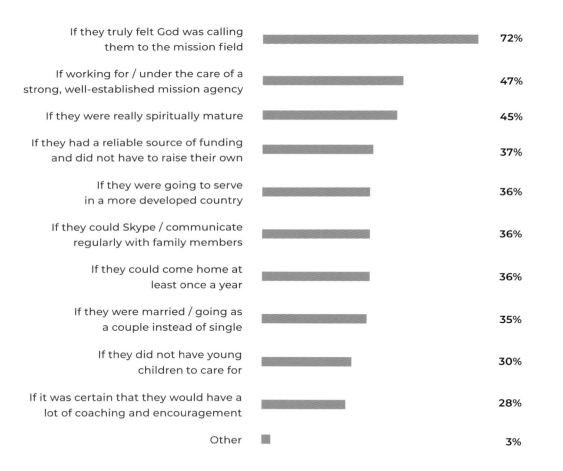

Factor	%
If they truly felt God was calling them to the mission field	72%
If working for / under the care of a strong, well-established mission agency	47%
If they were really spiritually mature	45%
If they had a reliable source of funding and did not have to raise their own	37%
If they were going to serve in a more developed country	36%
If they could Skype / communicate regularly with family members	36%
If they could come home at least once a year	36%
If they were married / going as a couple instead of single	35%
If they did not have young children to care for	30%
If it was certain that they would have a lot of coaching and encouragement	28%
Other	3%

n=504 U.S. engaged churchgoing Christian parents, Sept. 2019.

spiritual and mental health needs. I wanted to understand where he might need extra support."

- "There have been a handful of people over the years who've said things like, 'Oh, don't you worry about her?' or 'Are you disappointed she chose missions instead of a good job?' but I try to turn those conversations into a testimony about Jesus' provision. 'Isn't it incredible,' I say, 'that God meets every need?'"

- "We have family who aren't believers who support our son in his work. It's such an incredible opportunity to witness."

- "We couldn't have asked for a more supportive church. They wrote our son into the budget and consider him 'our missionary,' even though he didn't go with our denomination's sending organization."

- "Our church small group has been enormously encouraging. They support our daughter financially but, more importantly, in prayer. We pray together for her every week, and it means so much to me."

MISSIONS & YOU

- As you consider the young person or people in your sphere of influence whom God is calling into ministry, what strikes you about their parents? Are they "all in"? What kind of encouragement or reassurance (or challenge!) do they need?

- One IMB leader calls missionaries' parents "the first senders." What do you think about this image and idea?

- What kind of rituals (laying on of hands, anointing with oil, prayer times, etc.) could your community incorporate into its services to engage parents and families in the holy act of commissioning their children for God's service?

With the right kind of discipleship and ongoing support, parents can disciple and support the potential missionaries growing up in their home.

What Can We Do Now to Prepare the Next Generations for Missions?

G ood leaders find a sustainable tension between near-term needs and longer-term dreams and, because generational analysis offers a sense of where things are headed, using it wisely can help.

Good leaders also use the right tool for the task at hand—and there are some things generational analysis is not good for. It's useful, with caveats and qualifications, for perceiving big trends.

It's not good for analyzing individual people.

"OK, Boomer."

"Millennial snowflake."

(Gen X is the middle child no one remembers to insult.)

Whatever age cohort you're in, practice good leadership. Use the tool of generational analysis to help you understand these times and make wise decisions for the present and future. As you try to understand older and younger individuals in your church or organization (or family!), be humble. Ask questions. Listen well.

Why? To be more like Jesus, absolutely yes.

But also because the future of missions depends on it.

CHAPTER

10

The findings detailed in this report reveal significant differences between younger and older Christians when it comes to their perspectives on global missions. And in order to answer the questions raised here, it's got to be all hands on deck. We need all of us to prepare for the next 10, 20, 50 or 150 years of cross-cultural ministry.

In that spirit, here are 10 jumping-off points for wrestling with questions surrounding missions past, present and future.

1. Bridge the Gap

When it comes to what Christians value about missions and missionaries, there is broad agreement that humanitarian work in the name of Jesus is noble, good and worthy of financial support. There is less consensus, however, around evangelistic activities. Barna has identified "evangelism ambivalence" elsewhere (see, for example, *Reviving Evangelism* and *Spiritual Conversations in the Digital Age*), and it's not going away.

The reason it's not going away is this: Most people don't know how to both share the good news about Christ *and* be respectful and culturally sensitive. Why? Because it's hard. It's enormously difficult to separate the faith from one's culture and pass on only the faith. Missiologists have been wrestling with it since at least the time of Matteo Ricci in the seventeenth century, and exactly no one would say Christians always get this right.

There is a gap between wanting to share good news and understanding the ways in which it is still good news for people very different from us. Figuring out how to bridge the gap, in the company of younger and older believers, can help everyday engaged Christians wholeheartedly embrace the value of cross-cultural mission.

2. Deal with the Past

Part of the "figuring it out" must entail reckoning with the past. The law of unintended consequences is ironclad and inescapable: Even with the best of intentions—sharing the good news of Jesus! working to extend God's Kingdom!—our actions *will* have unanticipated effects. And as the data show, young adults are particularly sensitive to the ways missions has unintentionally brought more bad news than good.

Where missions efforts have gone wrong, we must confess and repent. Where it is possible, amends should be made. The AA classic *Twelve Steps and Twelve Traditions* says, "An honest regret for harms done, a genuine gratitude for blessings received, and a willingness to try for better things tomorrow will be the permanent assets we shall seek." It has the ring of Paul to the Corinthians: "Your sorrow led you to repentance. For you became sorrowful as God intended" (2 Cor. 7:9).

3. Pray & Teach Prayer

Time and again, Barna data on churches and Christian organizations confirm that communities of prayer are more likely to thrive—yet we see in *The Future of Missions* study some troubling indicators related to prayer. Young adults and teens are far less likely than older adults to say that praying specifically for missions is in their future. It's possible some of their reluctance will dissipate as churches wrestle together through missions-related concerns (see "Deal with the Past" above), but it's also possible young Christians need pastoral teaching on the importance of prayer and coaching on how to actually do it. Find out which is the case for your people and respond accordingly.

Meanwhile, don't forget to pray.

4. Preach the Whole Gospel

In research for David Kinnaman's book *Faith for Exiles*, Barna found that young Christians with a well-rounded, theologically rich understanding of the gospel are more likely to have a resilient, lasting faith—but also that such an understanding is uncommon among young believers. In order to dispel the dichotomy some perceive between aid and evangelism, Christians need a richer understanding of the gospel.

Those who want missions to major only on evangelism need a fuller gospel that includes God's call for his people to "do justice and love mercy" (Micah 6:8). Those who want missions to major only on humanitarian work need a fuller gospel that includes the Great Commission (Matthew 28:16–20). There is no dichotomy in the whole gospel.

5. Talk About Money

Open the floor to conversations around fundraising, accountability, digital tools and so on, so that the next generation of missions supporters can get fully invested. You don't have to solve it, but you can make it okay to talk about.

These conversations may not be comfortable; they may range further than you'd like (when was the last time you had to defend tax exemption for churches and religious nonprofits?). But, as data show time and again, institutional trust is at an unprecedented low. Leaders can't afford *not* to talk about money.

6. Connect with Missionaries

Knowing a missionary, as we've seen, is transformative when it comes to engagement with missions. If you do nothing else on this list, open the doors of your community to missionaries. They are missions with skin on! A close relationship and regular interactions with them will do more to rouse your church for global ministry than just about anything else could. And close connections will help keep everyone accountable to follow through on their part of the Kingdom work.

Once you've identified the missions-sensitive young people in your sphere of influence, work on connecting them at an individual level. Many current missionaries would like to mentor the workers of tomorrow, but need help getting connected—if you can, help make that happen.

7. Use Your Imagination

Barna polled four "new" kinds of missionaries—business leader, entrepreneur, artist, church trainer—but you don't have to stop there. "Tasha" from the introduction is a Hebrew teacher and mobile app developer. "Jim" is a farmer and English teacher. "Matt" is a videographer and graphic designer. "Greta" is a mom. "Jake" is a dentist. These profiles are based on real people serving God cross-culturally, and they can serve as inspiration for any young person wondering what kind of mission work they could do. Answer: Pretty much anything!

What kind of conversations can you lead to help people broaden their understanding of "missionary"?

8. Discern, Equip & Release

Barna has written many thousands of words about the importance of "vocational discipleship"—helping people connect the dots between their faith and their work. As churches have (often for good reason) shifted away from "pushing" ministry callings, young people who might have pursued vocational ministry have chased other dreams. But strong vocational discipleship leads Christ-followers to discern both their gifts *and* the Church's needs—and the Church needs tomorrow's leaders to discern God's call, get equipped and be released for ministry. Missions work is one aspect of that need.

Are you identifying and raising up the leaders who will one day replace you and others who are currently leading the global Church? Even (and perhaps especially) if you are young, the time to begin is now.

9. Disciple Parents

Most parents want the very best for their kids, but somewhere along the way, "the very best" got a little mixed up for Christians. The data indicate that some parents need, ahem, pastoral guidance in this area: As Barna found in research related to higher education, most Christian parents' goals for their children's future are indistinguishable from non-Christian parents'.

This is a discipleship problem.

What can you do to help parents reframe the work of raising kids into a calling to make disciples? If their family are engaged believers, no Christian teen or young adult should have to wonder what Mom or Dad will say when they receive God's call to the mission field.

10. Involve Everybody

Generational analysis is useful for understanding big trends, but intergenerational relationships are beneficial for just about everything else. Look around at your leadership team. Do you need to diversify when it comes to age, ethnicity or gender? Missions is a team sport, whether it's close to home or on the other side of the globe—so make sure you've got everybody on the literal or figurative field.

The questions raised by the data in this report must be answered *with* the next generation. *With* is what holds the people of God together through time and across miles.

Barna Voices on the Future of Missions

ALY HAWKINS

MANAGING EDITOR (TULSA, OK)

I'm 44, smack in the middle of Gen X, but like Millennials Erin and Julian Williams (page 62), my ambivalence toward missions comes from a place of deep love for the Church and for our mission to live and proclaim the good news of Christ's here-and-coming Kingdom. I count myself among the "older adult" supportive skeptics—with emphasis on *supportive*.

I have family and friends on the mission field—"Marion and James" from the introduction are a fictionalized version of my parents, and "Donna and Jim," from the missionary profile in chapter 4, are dear friends—and I donate monthly to an international missions organization. When my church's youth group has a bake sale to raise funds for a short-term trip, I can be trusted to overpay for baked goods (*mmmm*, banana bread), even though part of me feels squirmy about the wisdom of sending 15-year-olds to Panama in Jesus' name.

I'm fully on board with the Church's calling, yet I can't help but wonder if some of the ways we answer it make our mission harder in the long run.

There's a concept in Catholic social teaching, "subsidiarity," which contends that decisions that affect people's lives ought to be made as close to the ground as possible. (Local school boards are an example of subsidiarity. The U.S. Department of Education, less so.) I'm a proponent of "missions subsidiarity," if such a thing exists. I don't believe we know best for people thousands of miles and many cultures away. We serve Jesus and have discretionary

ALY HAWKINS and **VERÓNICA THAMES** are missionaries' kids who now work at Barna. Here they reflect on the research, their experiences, their own skepticism and their hopes for the future of cross-cultural ministry.

income, and I love that we want to share both with people who don't. But serving Jesus and spending money don't make us experts on how to do either of those things anywhere but where we are.

When I read *The Future of Missions* findings, I recognize many youngish Christians like me who are all in for Jesus and his global, multicultural Body. But we're checking ourselves before we put everything on the table for American-led missions. I'm encouraged and inspired by what I see and hear from believers around the world, and want anything we do from here to support and—where possible and appropriate—submit to their close-to-the-ground leadership.

VERÓNICA THAMES
ASSOCIATE EDITOR (NASHVILLE, TN)

Missions holds a special place in my heart, and I recognize its importance—after all, Jesus did say, "Go and make disciples of all nations" (Matthew 28:19, NIV). But at the same time, there are parts of the Western missions strategy that, despite being widely accepted, cause me and many others to second guess the intentions behind the actions.

As a Millennial who spent the majority of her teen years living on the mission field, returning to the States for college gave me enough distance to process my thoughts on global missions, and especially missions to the unreached. I've always had mixed feelings about being a missionary's kid and, after reading *The Future of Missions*, have learned I'm not alone in my opinions on global evangelism.

My experience with overseas missions shaped who I am today, but it is also because of this experience that I feel compelled to examine how the Church's approach to global evangelism can hurt more than help. Like many of my peers, I wonder about the traditional methods of raising support, and am disheartened by the pain and cultural disconnect caused by centuries of misplaced missions efforts. I long to see a change in the way future generations approach missions, especially when it comes to diversifying those who are invested in, equipped for and eventually sent into the mission field.

While these changes will not happen overnight, findings from *The Future of Missions* show that difficult questions are being asked *now*, sparking conversations that will hopefully refine the Church's approach. Data reveal that half of young-adult Christians (52%) qualify as potential missionaries, one-quarter of whom are supportive skeptics like me (26%). It's encouraging to know that most of us still affirm the importance of sharing our faith with others and want to find a way to do that effectively *and* responsibly.

As stated on page 60, relationships play a major role in shaping personal opinions. For young Christians, relationships inform our perspective of missions and also serve as accountability for ourselves and our peers. I think this is a wonderful reminder that, in order to see more people enter into a relationship with Christ, we need to be in constant relationship with him and with other believers, seeking and submitting to his guidance as we seek to guide others toward him.

A. Endnotes

1   See, for example, Christopher Allen, "Missions and the Mediation of Modernity in Colonial Kenya," *Penn History Review* 20, No. 1, (Spring 2013). https://repository.upenn.edu/cgi/viewcontent.cgi?article=1063&context=phr (accessed March 2020).

2   David Kinnaman and Gabe Lyons, *Good Faith: Being a Christian When Society Thinks You're Irrelevant and Extreme* (Grand Rapids, MI: Baker Books, 2016).

3   Barna FaithView Database [accessed March 10, 2020] https://barna.juiceboxdata.com/barna_faith/

4   See, for example, David King, "How Religion Motivates People to Give and Serve," *The Conversation*, Aug. 19, 2017. http://theconversation.com/how-religion-motivates-people-to-give-and-serve-81662 (accessed March 2020).

5   @charlotteirene8, "Missionary work is a form of colonization and inherently racist," Twitter, July 19, 2018, 4:54 a.m., https://twitter.com/charlotteirene8/status/1019913286958112768?lang=en.

6   From an informal poll of the managing editor's Facebook friends.

7   Barna Group, *Reviving Evangelism* (Ventura, CA: Barna Group, 2019); Barna Group, *Spiritual Conversations in the Digital Age* (Ventura, CA: Barna Group, 2018).

8   "Matteo Ricci, SJ (1552–1610)," Ignatian Spirituality, n.d., https://www.ignatianspirituality.com/ignatian-voices/16th-and-17th-century-ignatian-voices/matteo-ricci-sj/ (accessed March 2020).

9   Congregation for the Doctrine of the Faith, International Theological Commission, "Faith and Inculturation," 1998, http://www.vatican.va/roman_curia/congregations/cfaith/cti_documents/rc_cti_1988_fede-inculturazione_en.html.

10   For example, *The Open Secret* (1978), *Foolishness to the Greeks* (1986) and *The Gospel in a Pluralist Society* (1989).

11   From an informal poll of the managing editor's Facebook friends.

12   Barna Group, *The Generosity Gap* (Ventura, CA: Barna Group, 2017).

13   Barna Group, *The Good News About Global Poverty* (Ventura, CA: Barna Group, 2018), 100.

14   S.C. Wright, A. Aron, T. McLaughlin-Volpe, and S.A. Ropp, "The Extended Contact Effect: Knowledge of Cross-group Friendships and Prejudice," *Journal of Personality and Social Psychology*, 73 No. 1, 73–90, https://doi.org/10.1037/0022-3514.73.1.73 (accessed March 2020).

15   Matthew Swayne, "How Knowing Just One Gay Person Can Shift Our Attitude Toward Equality," *World Economic Forum*, December 18, 2018, https://www.weforum.org/agenda/2018/12/knowing-just-one-gay-person-shifts-attitudes/ (accessed March 2020).

16   Barna Group, "Americans Soften on Immigration in 2017," September 19, 2017, https://www.barna.com/research/americans-soften-immigration-2017/ (accessed March 2020).

17   Barna Group, *The Good News About Global Poverty*.

18   Barna Group, *What's Next for Biblical Higher Education* (Ventura, CA: Barna Group, 2017)

19   Alcoholics Anonymous, *Twelve Steps and Twelve Traditions* (Alcoholics Anonymous World Services, 2002), p. 95.

B. Methodology

The findings from this study emerged from 3,606 online interviews with U.S. self-identified Christians, including 1,500 adults 35 and older (all engaged Protestants, see definitions below), 1,000 younger adults 18 to 34 (856 engaged Protestants), 602 teenagers 13 to 17 (380 engaged Protestants) and 504 engaged Protestant parents of children 13 to 25. Barna also interviewed 633 U.S. Protestant pastors of missions-focused churches. Older adults, younger adults and teen interviews were conducted December 11, 2018 to January 8, 2019. Engaged Christian parents were interviewed September 11–27, 2019, and pastors were interviewed January 8–20, 2019. Margins of error are as follows, all at the 95% confidence level:

- Adults 35 and older: ±2.3 percentage points
- Younger adults 18 to 24: ±3.2 percentage points
- Teens 13 to 17: ±4.9 percentage points
- Parents: ±4.3 percentage points
- Pastors: ±3.8 percentage points

Engaged Protestants have attended a Protestant church at least once within the past month, are involved in their church in more ways that attending services, have made a commitment to Jesus that is still important in their life today and say their faith is very important in the life today.

Barna researchers also interviewed 16 current missionaries from August to October 2019. Each interview was 45 to 60 minutes. Identifying details have been changed to protect them, their families and their ministries.

Definitions

Engaged churchgoing Christians, sometimes called engaged Christians in this report for the sake of brevity, attend a Protestant church at least once a month, say they are involved with their church in more ways than just attending services, have made a commitment to Jesus that is important in their life today and say their religious faith is very important in their life today. Age groups:

- Teens 13 to 17
- Young adults 18 to 34
- Older adults 35 and older

Other engaged Christians, sometimes called *non-churchgoers* in this report, otherwise qualify as engaged but are not regular churchgoers.

Engaged Christian parents are engaged Christians who have at least one child age 13 to 25.

Potential missionaries say they would "definitely" be interested in serving as one or more of four different missionary profiles (see ch. 8).

Ethnicity is based on self-identification.

Supportive skeptics:

- Have donated money to missions
- Don't think missionary work is "very" valuable *or* are bothered by evangelism
- Agree strongly or somewhat with one or more of the following statements:

- Missions work can sometimes lead to unhealthy local dependence on charity.
- Charity work often hurts the local economy.
- Christianity should fix its reputation before doing more missions.
- Christian mission is tainted by its association with colonialism.

Acknowledgments

The Barna team offers our deepest thanks to our partners at the International Mission Board, especially Paul Chitwood, John Brady, Lukas Naugle, Bryson Holston, Julie McGowan, Chris Kennedy, Leslie Caldwell and so many others. We also want to thank our generous contributors, whose insights do so much to bring the numbers to life: Karen Huber, Barbara Jones, Erin and Julian Williams and the missionaries and missionary parents who shared their experiences.

The research team for *The Future of Missions* is David Kinnaman, Brooke Hempell, Savannah Kimberlin, Janet Eason, Aidan Dunn, Pam Jacob and Aly Hawkins. Under the editorial direction of Alyce Youngblood, Aly Hawkins wrote the report with help from Verónica Thames. Doug Brown edited the manuscript. Traci Hochmuth and Aly Hawkins created the data visualizations, which were designed, along with the full report, by Annette Allen. With creative direction from Joe Jensen, DayCloud Studios designed the cover. Mallory Holt and Elissa Clouse managed the project while Brenda Usery managed production. *The Future of Missions* team thanks our Barna colleagues Amy Brands, Daniel Copeland, Kristin Jackson, Steve McBeth, Rhesa Storms, Jess Villa and Todd White.

About the Project Partners

Barna Group is a research firm dedicated to providing actionable insights on faith and culture, with a particular focus on the Christian church. In its 35-year history, Barna has conducted more than one million interviews in the course of hundreds of studies, and has become a go-to source for organizations that want to better understand a complex and changing world from a faith perspective.

Barna's clients and partners include a broad range of academic institutions, churches, nonprofits and businesses, such as Alpha, the Templeton Foundation, Fuller Seminary, the Bill and Melinda Gates Foundation, Maclellan Foundation, DreamWorks Animation, Focus Features, Habitat for Humanity, The Navigators, NBC-Universal, the ONE Campaign, Paramount Pictures, the Salvation Army, Walden Media, Sony and World Vision. The firm's studies are frequently quoted by major media outlets such as *The Economist*, BBC, CNN, *USA Today,* the *Wall Street Journal*, Fox News, Huffington Post, *The New York Times* and the *Los Angeles Times*.

www.Barna.com

The International Mission Board (IMB) is the 175-year-old global missionary-sending entity of the Southern Baptist Convention. Since its beginning in 1845, the IMB has had one goal: to take the gospel of Jesus Christ to the lost people of the world. The vision that drives the work of the International Mission Board is drawn from Revelation 7:9–10: the vision of realizing "a multitude from every language, people, tribe and nation knowing and worshiping our Lord Jesus Christ" (ESV).

IMB's mission is to serve Southern Baptists in carrying out the Great Commission to make disciples of all nations. Through the IMB, Southern Baptists and global partners are mobilized to pray for those who have yet to hear the gospel, to give to support their nearly 4,000 full-time missionaries around the globe and to send and support those from their churches who feel compelled to go on mission. Our strategic anchors for that work include advancing the missionary task among unreached peoples and places, advancing relationships with Southern Baptists and global partners, and advancing the efficiency and effectiveness of our global operations.

www.IMB.org